Faith and Victory in Dachau

Faith and Victory in Dachau

by

Rev. Jack Overduin

PAIDEIA PRESS
St. Catharines, Ontario, Canada

First published in Dutch as *Hel en Hemel van Dachau*, ©
J.H. Kok of Kampen. Translated by Harry der Nederlanden.

Illustrations by Don Spencer.

ISBN 0-88815-901-3
Printed in the United States of America.

Table of Contents

Foreword

This is not a book about a hero.

Yet it is a heroic book.

Rev. Jack Overduin warns against the danger of viewing him as a hero; he wants to give all honor to the grace of Christ. Yet this part of his life's story brings to mind the words of the Letter to the Hebrews: "By faith Moses chose to share ill-treatment with the people of God . . . . by faith he suffered abuse for the Christ . . ." (Heb. 11:25,26). The power of faith became manifest in that unique time in that particular situation. In order to understand and learn from it, we need some background information.

The setting was the rape of the Netherlands by Nazi Germany. A free country was violated and trampled down by a totalitarian power.

It happened on the tenth day of May 1940.

On that beautiful spring day, German bombers and fighter planes attacked Holland while ground troops invaded the Low Countries in famous blitzkrieg fashion. The Dutch soldiers defended their country bravely, but were no match for the better-equipped enemy.

When on May fourteenth the flames of Rotterdam,

7

bombed to ruins, rose to heaven and other major cities were
threatened with a similar disaster, army and government
capitulated. For a long time freedom was gone.

Holland had been a country of freedom for centuries. Each
individual worshipped God in accordance with his own conscience. There were many organizations, a free press,
freedom of religion and independent schools.

Many of these independent schools were Christian day
schools. They had been founded in the nineteenth century by
parents who made great sacrifices to enable their children to
be educated in obedience to the Word of God. Since 1918
these schools, like all others in the Netherlands, were fi-
nanced by the government.

Freedom! The only atmosphere in which a Dutchman
could breathe was that of freedom.

But freedom in a totalitarian state does not exist.
Everything and everyone must be subservient to the state; the
state alone rules and organizes. The family as well as the
school becomes subservient to the state. There is only one
social movement, and it is directed by the state. Churches are
free to speak about God who rules in heaven, but not about a
sovereign God who rules over all things on earth.

On the fifteenth day of May, 1940, the Netherlands lost its
political freedom. From that day on they were to lose all their
freedoms.

Hitler appointed an Austrian, Dr. Seyss Inquart, to be
governor of the Netherlands.

This man delivered a speech on May 29, 1940, in which he
spoke of his desire to maintain good relations with all Dutchmen. He referred to "ties of blood" and said: "Today we
feel responsible for the right and pure blood everywhere, for
blood obliges in spite of external facts and lack of insight."
Persons of the right Nordic blood were good people, and persons of the wrong blood—like the Jews—were bad people.
The man was a racist, and the Nazi doctrine was a racist doctrine.

Only a small group of Dutchmen, organized as the so-called National Socialists (N.S.B.), agreed with this racist theory. But what a *temptation* it was for many to accept the invitation of the German governor to cooperate as much as possible, and thereby avoiding all conflict. We have heard the slogan, "Better red than dead." The Dutchmen of that day were tempted to say, "Better brown* than down." By far the majority of Dutchmen resisted that temptation, however. Immediately, underground as well as public resistance was formed. The underground resistance acted in many ways: it hid Jews and allied pilots, printed illegal papers, and engaged in sabotage. Public resistance was especially visible and audible in churches and schools that refused to capitulate to the Nazi system.

Every Sunday many church leaders prayed for the legal government, especially for Queen Wilhelmina and the royal house. Several ministers were arrested simply for such intercession. They were imprisoned, deported, and some paid the price of their life. But that prayer was a public sign during those five years of occupation, a sign that the spirit of a free people cannot be broken. New meaning became evident in old psalms, the Hebrew songs of liberation. The sermons comforted and strengthened the people. Several times messages were read from the pulpits in which Roman Catholic and Protestant churches unanimously protested against the inhuman practices of the Nazis.

One of the first churchmen to fearlessly encourage his fellow Christians was Prof. K. Schilder of Kampen. In June 1940 already he wrote about the obedience owing to the legal government of Queen Wilhelmina and about the ongoing duty to combat National Socialism. A man small of stature but great of courage was the Roman Catholic priest and professor Titus Brandsma who died in Dachau, and whose Jesus poem is quoted by Rev. Overduin on page 155.

---

*The shirts of the Nazis were brown.

And so we come to Rev. (Jack) Overduin who wrote this book.

Nobody could have predicted that Rev. Overduin would become one of the major figures to publicly resist the Nazis, for he was not a militant man. He was always busy in the work of evangelism and extremely gifted in translating the Gospel, in terms of his time, for the unchurched. He was a man of peace who encouraged good manners and Christian culture, a Christian gentleman.

This man was plunged into the school conflict in Arnhem. He did not yield an inch; he stood his ground, showing himself to be a man of strong Biblical faith.

That seemingly small local conflict at Arnhem might have had the gravest consequences. It was a test case. If the Nazi authorities could have succeeded in taking over and transforming this one Christian school, the ranks of Christians would have been broken, and the enemy would have applied the same satanic tactics in other schools. If Rev. Overduin had changed the content of his sermon on that decisive Sunday morning because he saw a Gestapo agent sitting in his congregation, *he* might have remained bodily free; but the school and the spirit of the people would have been imprisoned.

However, Overduin was faithful to God, and the Lord was faithful to him. The fascinating story of that faithfulness is recorded in this volume.

On the morning of the day I wrote this introduction, I heard on the radio that American Nazis were allowed to organize a march in Chicago. Such an announcement makes the content of this book particularly relevant. More significant, however, is the fact that totalitarianism did not become extinct after the demise of the German Nazis; concentration camps were not abolished after the closing of Dachau.

There is no human freedom or Christian liberty in the Soviet Union and its satellite states; in Cuba or Red China.

DACHAU, AUSCHWITZ, THE GULAG ARCHIPELAGO....

The idols of the Nazis were the Führer and the Nordic race; the idols of communism are Marx and Lenin and the anticipated classless society. Idols demand sacrifices; they require the bodies and souls of men.

There are still concentration camps, described by Alexander Solzhenitsyn as a vast system of islands which he calls *The Gulag Archipelago,* ranging from the heart of European Russia to the wastelands of Siberia:

> This Archipelago crisscrossed and patterned that other country within which it was located, like a gigantic patchwork, cutting into its cities, hovering over its streets. Yet there were many who did not even guess at its presence and many, many others who had heard something vague. And only those who had been there knew the whole truth (p. X).

Solzhenitsyn was there, and wants us to be informed; Overduin was there during the Nazi occupation and does not want us to forget.

We need to be instructed in the ideology and the practice of the totalitarian powers of our time, so that we may "test the spirits to see whether they are of God" (I John 4:1) and "to take the whole armor of God, that we may be able to withstand in the evil day, and having done all, to stand" (Eph. 6:13).

May this book of Overduin be widely read in the school of freedom, of genuine Christian freedom.

Louis Praamsma

The Conflict

In Arnhem stood the attractive Van Loben Sels School, perhaps one of the most beautiful school buildings in the Netherlands, its beauty enhanced by an equally picturesque setting. But inside this beautiful school was a cankerous spot. One of the teachers was a traitor. His colleagues were already suspicious of him prior to May 1940, but like many others, he feigned total innocence. However, when the time was ripe, when he felt behind him the strength of the bayonets of the enemy (his friends) and the power of the Gestapo, he dropped his mask.

The design of the Nazis for this man was obvious. One way or another, the head of the school, Mr. J.M. Caspers, was to be removed and replaced by an enemy-indoctrinated teacher. Gradually, therefore, the Christian school would be reduced to a propaganda institution for National Socialism. The staff would be forced to cooperate under threats of purge.

The situation in Arnhem was not, of course, an isolated instance. A general order had been issued in The Hague, the enemy's administrative capital, to get control of the schools, and especially the Christian schools, which were not in the hands of the state but were directed by parent-controlled boards.

Publications have since appeared which analyze the fight
for freedom of existence by the schools and churches during
the German occupation. Through the study of official
documents and circulars, among other things, a comprehensive picture emerges of the Nazi attack on the spiritual
freedom of the schools and churches, and also of the final
frustration and resignation of the Nazis. For one to get an
idea of the conflict in Arnhem as part of the national conflict,
some knowledge is required of the tactics that were used to
break the power and influence of Christian education. The
strategy was to render the local school boards and national
organizations impotent by depriving them of almost all their
power or by subjecting that power to the supervision of the
state.

First, the power of the local school boards to hire teachers
and to supervise and judge the principial, practical, and
professional competency of teachers was transferred to The
Hague, to the Department of Education where the word of
the German authorities was supreme. The appointment and
hiring of personnel had to be approved by the Department.
With its power of veto, The Hague could then impose unwant-
ed teachers on the school boards and parents. It was a choice
of either submitting or losing subsidy and having the entire
system of Christian education collapse through financial
failure. Stubborn school boards could be disbanded by
Hague officials and replaced with a commissioner who was
an ally of the new order. The plan was, even at this point, to
begin empowering commissioners as supervisors over the
school boards.

In Arnhem, the conflict grew very sharp. Because conditions seemed favorable there, that city apparently was to
serve as the proving ground for the process of assimilation in
all the schools. The Nazis already had a traitor inside the
school, a schemer who was willing to get ahead at the cost of
fellow teachers and students. Moreover, Gestapo headquarters were close at hand, and serving there were several Dutch
turncoats who had themselves attended Christian schools but

who had since turned in hatred against everything Christian.

One of these was the Gestapo agent Zylstra, a dangerous person who had the callousness to interrogate me even though before the war he had spent many an hour in my study discussing various of his problems. He was one of those who had sought asylum in the National Socialist Movement, many of whom suffered from unrestrained megalomania, seeing themselves as superior beings who were prevented from getting ahead and gaining recognition only because of the decadence of democracy. For someone like Zylstra, following common educational routes and achieving knowledge and insight through years of intellectual effort and willpower was beneath his dignity. Men like Zylstra tell themselves that they have already reached that height. Among other things, Zylstra did considerable harm in the school conflict at Arnhem.

The methods of the Gestapo and of the Nazi regime were highly refined. Even the most insidious activities could be justified by law. For example, in order to depose and punish someone, a conflict was precipitated which would provide legal ground for such action. Such people did not just come out and say, "We want headmaster Caspers out of the way because he is loyal to the principles of the school, and we want to replace him with our own man," for that would awaken the people to what was happening. When Caspers was dismissed, the people had to be able to say: "It was his own fault. Why did he have to be so obtuse? How could he show so little insight into the new order of things, risking not only his own freedom but also that of the school?"

To achieve this dismissal, a war of nerves was initiated. The Nazi turncoat Veenstra, quibbled, sabotaged, and provoked wherever he could, hoping that the headmaster would react in such a way that he could register a complaint against him. Even prior to the war, Veenstra had been, generally speaking, difficult to work with, both for his colleagues and for the headmaster. He had always been critical of the students, the parents, the administration, and the government, but that criticism became more vicious and more outspoken as May 1940 approached. He had already been heard saying, "If the Germans invade our country, we should not resist." And although he continued to deny that he was part of the National Socialist Movement, he began to defend that movement more and more.

When the German invasion had been accomplished, Mr. Caspers, the headmaster, asked each teacher individually, "Can we continue to work with one another in full trust, without anyone's raising obstacles, or must we adopt reservations toward one another?" Everyone, including Veenstra, opted for the former, and during the following months, Veenstra expressed his contempt for informers and berated such meanness.

Nevertheless, relationships amongst the teaching staff grew increasingly tense. Veenstra defended the Nazi conscription of young men to work in Germany, the closing of the schools to Jewish children, and other innovations of National Socialism. He continually found a principial opponent in Mr. Caspers. Soon, too, the parents of the students also began to realize that something was amiss. In the fall of 1940, Caspers confronted Veenstra with the question: "Are you or aren't you a member of the National Socialist Movement? The parents of your students have been asking." Veenstra was livid and entered a complaint against Caspers with the school board.

Beginning in January 1941, whenever a conflict developed between Veenstra and the administration, the former threatened that he had the backing of certain authorities. In April of 1941, he announced that he was a member of the "Teacher's Guild," and at the same time he warned the headmaster and staff that the school had a bad name in "Utrecht" (headquarters). To the sceptical questions of the headmaster, Veenstra replied that the reports spoke of "a school in an eastern city." The propaganda posters of the National Socialist Movement shortly thereafter appeared in Veenstra's windows.

After the summer vacation of 1941, Veenstra grew bolder

and advised Caspers to "orient the school to the direction set by the new order." When this was vigorously rebuffed, Veenstra began to threaten Mr. Caspers. Caspers told him that he was responsible only to the school board and that, if demands were made on him contrary to his conscience, he would be unable to bear the responsibility any longer, and he would resign his position.

A few weeks later, Veenstra set the trap that was to catch Headmaster Caspers. On the blackboard of his classroom Veenstra wrote: "With Germany—against Bolshevism." The next day the headmaster asked him, "Do you think it wise, what you wrote on the blackboard? It explicitly introduces politics into the classroom and among the students— something which you yourself have constantly condemned." Veenstra's reply was a meaningful grin. Mr. Caspers had taken the bait. He had dared to challenge the sacred slogan, an act which could not go unpunished.

On November 27, while Mr. Caspers was sick in bed, the security police came to pick him up. They searched his house from attic to cellar. Mr. Caspers was told to report to Nazi headquarters as soon as he was well. He went two weeks later, and heard two charges brought against him. The first, regarding the slogan on the blackboard, accused him of having said that such a statement was outrageous. Second, to a student leaving school to become a painter, he was accused of having said, "Do your best, son. Maybe one day you'll become Führer." (In his early days Adolf Hitler had aspired to be a painter.) Mr. Caspers could reply with a clear conscience that the first charge was a distortion of his words, and that the second was a complete fabrication.

Veenstra was called and faced the headmaster as the accuser. On the desk lay a complete dossier against Mr. Caspers—a testimony against Veenstra's earlier assurance that he could be trusted and that he condemned informers. The next day, December 11, Mr. Caspers again had to appear before the security police to face the same charges.

Mr. Caspers continued to deny the accusation by responding thus: "Even if you ask me the same thing ten times, you'll only get the same answer you got yesterday." He was immediately imprisoned. By God's blessing, his imprisonment in the House of Detention lasted only one month.

The school was thus left without a headmaster. However, the headmaster from the one other Christian school in the district was appointed temporary head of the Arnhem school. But Veenstra also intimidated the new headmaster mercilessly and the latter was permitted to return to his own school at his request.

Shortly after his imprisonment, the board received orders from the Nazi-controlled Department of Education in The Hague to deny Mr. Caspers entrance to his school. Immediately there followed a German order to dismiss Mr. Caspers for inflammatory propaganda against the Third Reich. The board never carried out this order, but it did think it wise to appoint someone else as temporary headmaster. Ready to assume the difficult and dangerous position was Mr. van den Berg, on furlough from Indonesia.

At the end of January, the school board dismissed Veenstra for his attitude toward various board members and for his refusal to cooperate with the new headmaster appointed by the board. The dismissal of Veenstra by the board can, at least in part, be credited to the board's obtaining the services of Mr. Meyerink, a former member of the government, as its advisor.

There followed a complicated and confused struggle between the school board on one side and Veenstra, the security police, and the Department of Education, on the other. The school was closed, reopened, and then closed again, sometimes by order of the Germans, and at other times by order of the school board. When the enemy opened the school, few or none of the students and none of the staff except Veenstra showed up; when the school board opened the school, everyone came.

For the dismissal of Veenstra, Mr. Boersma, the school board vice president and Mr. Ploeger, its secretary, who were reckoned to be the strongest and most principial opposition, were thrown into jail. This occurred at the end of January, 1941. Their imprisonment lasted eight weeks. As a result of sickness and resignations, only five members were left on the board—just enough legally to continue making decisions. These five men together with Mr. Meyerink and the two headmasters met night after night under tremendous pressures, and in spite of constant danger to their own freedom. The complexion of the struggle changed continually so that new counter measures had to be constantly devised.

Because these events are related here as briefly as possible, it all sounds much simpler than it was. But the situation made severe demands on these men: living day and night in fear of arrest, they nevertheless persisted in their work.

Providing good leadership in the conflict and directing it to the right end was difficult for the school board because it had to deal with three hostile authorities, as well as Veenstra. However, each of these authorities guarded its own reputation and prestige, offering Meyerink (the board's advisor) the opportunity to play off one hostile authority against the other in order to focus the school's battle on a single enemy. The Department of Education was selected as the best one to deal with. It had appointed a Mr. Noordyk to deal with the school.

At the beginning of February, the order came that the school and its personnel had to submit to the leadership of Veenstra and that the school had to be immediately reopened. Both the staff and the board were called before the security police and told that failure to cooperate would be regarded as sabotage, which was punishable by firing squad. A short period was allowed for the threat to sink in. The parents were also informed of the peril of their actions; they too would be subject to severe punishment if their children did not return to school.

These threats caused great consternation. "What do we do now?" the Christians asked. "Must we be willing to die over this?" Many parents had no idea what to do. They were afraid and uncertain. Many of them came to me, as their pastor, for advice. I had only one thing to tell them: "Don't, under any conditions, sacrifice your children to the betrayer and to the enemy. A school under Veenstra is no longer a Christian school. We must be faithful; don't break your ranks in fear and a desire for self-preservation. Now is the time that we will have to put Christ's teaching into practice: 'He who wishes to be my disciple, let him take up his cross and follow me.' We may not desert the board and staff! We must take a unified stand, for their risk is greater than ours. It would be cowardice for the parents to collude with the enemy. It would be like stabbing these loyal men in the back!"

A very tense week passed. The Gestapo wanted to triumph over us, to bring us to heel. Did we dare to keep saying "No"? The people needed strength. And they had to find it at its source, in Jesus Christ. The following Sunday, therefore, as minister of the Gospel, I had to provide clear direction.

The conflict had reached a crisis. Mr. Caspers had been dismissed as head of the school, two board members had been thrown in jail, and Veenstra, the traitor, was head of the school. We knew that not all the children in the school came from Christian families of strong convictions. Could we count on all the parents? Many were terrified, for the Gestapo had threatened severe punishment to parents who dared to keep their children home. But these parents realized, too, that such passive resistance would upset the Nazis' devilishly ingenious plans for assimilating the Christian schools. Now as pastor, I had to speak a word. Not just a few generalizations, but a very concrete word. A grave decision confronted me.

The remaining school board members and several strong brothers visited the parents, going from home to home to remind them of their Christian duty as pledged at the baptism of their children. "Keep your children at home" was the word. Many parents stood firm, others wavered, a few were terror-stricken. It was, therefore, no wonder that the people of my church needed support and direction from the Word of God. The following week would be a decisive one. Would the parents, the school board, and the staff be forced to bend before the might and terror of violence and nihilism? The council of churches had, coincidentally, set aside that Sunday as a day of prayer for Christian education. For, as I have said, the future looked bleak for the freedom of all Christian action and especially for the Christian schools in the Netherlands. War had been declared on the whole enterprise of Christian education. The churches, therefore, felt the need to bring their distress and danger before the Lord and to pray for His deliverance. This trouble was epidemic in the Netherlands, but it was especially so in Arnhem, where the Nazi offensive had been launched.

We were confronted by a very visible, existential conflict. The people did not need any more generalities from the church, but they did want to have a specific course of Christian action pointed out for them, as simply and Scripturally as possible.

Because my wife would be directly involved in the consequences, I asked her, several days before the crucial Sunday of February 8, whether she agreed that I should proclaim a concrete and unambiguous word from the pulpit, and if she were prepared to endure the possible consequences of my imprisonment. Her answer was short: "What we need today are men, not cowards," but it was long enough for me to know that I could count on her spiritual and moral support. I had expected no less.

Sunday morning, February 8, I preached on Matthew 5:11,12: "Blessed are you when men revile you and persecute you and utter all kinds of evil against you falsely on my account. Rejoice and be glad, for your reward is great in heaven, for so men persecuted the prophets who were before you." After I had spoken the votum and blessing and was announcing the first song, two late-comers entered: Zylstra, the security police interrogator, and another Gestapo agent.

Now I was certain that things did not look promising for

me. I asked God for strength and faithfulness to deliver the sermon without omitting the dangerous passages. I could temper the sermon a bit in its delivery and make it a little less specific in order to avoid giving them the rope with which to hang me. Yet to have surrendered to this temptation at a time when the congregation was hungering for words of strength, would have been a betrayal of the Gospel and unfaithfulness to my Sender and the flock entrusted to me. But the Lord removed my fear and apprehension, and I preached with boldness and conviction.

I felt myself carried along by the prayers of the congregation—they did not abandon me—and by the prayers of our heavenly High Priest, "who in every respect has been tempted as we are, yet without sin" and who in His testimony before His enemies and persecutors "made the good confession." All bravado on the pulpit comes from satan. We may never entertain people with our daredeviltry and clever double-talk against the enemy. Especially at times such as this, there are always a few people who come to church for excitement. And if the minister isn't daring enough and doesn't satisfy their appetite for sensation, they immediately stand ready with destructive criticism. Although they demand little of themselves, they demand much from others. But this doesn't negate the fact that there are times and situations when so much is at stake that one must speak, when to be silent or to equivocate would be cowardice and sin. At such times we may be sure that we are not being reckless, but, rather, faithful. Then we are ready to accept all the consequences of witnessing against injustice in the name of Christ.

In the introduction of my sermon, I reminded the congregation that the entire country was that day observing a day of prayer for Christian education, which was in great danger. That danger was particularly acute in Arnhem. Therefore, as Christians, we in Arnhem had an urgent need to seek God's will in prayer. We all knew that brother Caspers had been imprisoned and that he had been dismissed as head of the school, while someone else—someone who was not one of us—had been forced upon us to take his place. And we also knew that two members of the school board were still in prison. I continued, saying it was therefore fitting that in our persecution and oppression we as Christian parents should find our comfort and strength in Christ, who made wonderful promises to those who are persecuted for the sake of righteousness. Only then could we follow the right road to martyrdom, for then martyrdom would not be invited by our own recklessness, but would be laid on us by Christ.

In the sermon I further pointed out that we can count on the fulfillment of the Word of salvation only if we are persecuted and reviled for the sake of righteousness. In deference to the powerful Word, we should first assume a respectful distance. The man who gets into conflict with the world on his own account or on account of stupidity is not declared blessed—only the man who knows that the cause is God's will have His favor.

What about the conflict in which we find ourselves? I asked. Is it really for Christ's sake? Has it been blown out of proportion by a stiff-necked school board, a hard-headed staff, and self-willed parents? We had to answer these questions, I told them, so that we ourselves were certain that we were standing on the promises of God in our persecution. For the answer, I pointed to the sacrament of baptism and the "Yes" the parents had spoken for their children at that time. We had promised before God that we would bring up our children and have them educated in the teachings of Christ.

Children belong to their parents, not to the state, and because these children have been baptized, I said, only Christ has a right to them; no one else. No one has the right to rob us of our children. God has entrusted them to us, and we as parents are responsible for their nurture. I told my congregation that no one but God could make a choice that would arbitrarily determine their future. The state did not make baptismal vows before the face of God. The parents did.

Because I was convinced of the divine seriousness of rightly
rearing children and of the heavy responsibility that parents
bear in the judgment of God, I said that it was possible for
us, as parents, to withstand the judgments of other men, for
those are merely human judgments. Here I adapted the words
of Luther, who said in one of the most critical moments of his
life: "It is better not to undertake something against one's
conscience." For these parents to support a school that was
no longer a Christian school controlled by the parents, and
for them to send their children there was contrary to their
conscience because it violated their baptismal vows and was
therefore contrary to the Word of God. Better for them to
tremble before the Word of the Lord than before the word of
man, no matter how powerful man may be.

He who is, in this sense, ready for persecution and
repression, vilification and scorn—for the world is not willing
to understand Scriptural motives—can be assured of the
blessing of the Lord. What a wonderful design Christ lays out
before those faithful disciples who confess Him! These are
the people who are lifted up above all human tragedy, I continued. Superficially speaking, we are tempted to call them
poor wretches, for they have to suffer innocently for the sake
of righteousness! Poor Mr. Boersma and Mr. Ploeger (school
board members), you are sitting in jail, although innocent,
for the good cause of our spiritual freedom!

No, says Christ, not poor wretches, but blessed! Congrat-
ulations! Happy and honored are you, Boersma, and you,
Ploeger!

Rejoice and be glad! We are being led into a wonderful
world, a world completely closed to flesh and blood. It is the
world of the Kingdom of Heaven which is open only to those
born again. Such suffering also opens a book written in a
heavenly language understood only by the children of God, I
told my congregation that day. The language is called
foolishness and is offensive to all who speak only in their
native tongue, in the language of the natural man.

But the new man, however, understands the language well

and says "Amen!" to Christ's "Blessed are you . . ." and to
His "Rejoice and be glad . . . ." We can then, and only then,
experience our oneness with all believers, with all the martyrs
of all ages. And we are enabled to reach out to all the
prophets who saw through the times of oppression and
misery to the imperishable Kingdom, which is reserved for us
as a gift of God's grace.

At the conclusion of my sermon, we sang two verses from a
well-known hymn by Martin Luther:*

> We do not build on earthly power
> which lasts but for a moment;
> we find our only strength in Him,
> whom God has made our Leader.
> You ask who that could be?
> His name is Christ the Lord,
> God's only begotten Son,
> the Victor on the throne,
> for He has won God's blessing.
>
> God's Word will stand eternally;
> His voice will never waver.
> Quake, Satan, for our Captain comes
> to scatter all your forces.
> Take family and friends,
> take goods and life away,
> you'll never take the throne,
> for Heaven is our own,
> and heirs are we to Kingdoms.

---

*These verses are an almost-literal rendition of the Dutch verses of "A
Mighty Fortress." The traditional English version does not quite bring out
the themes that Overduin wishes to emphasize in this context.

Arrest and Interrogation

After the delivery of the sermon, the consistory was afraid—and rightly so—that I would be arrested. It was heartening to see that everyone, nevertheless, seconded the sermon wholeheartedly. If the consistory had even partially blamed the consequences to recklessness on my part, my morale would have suffered a severe blow.

In order to present a complete picture, it is necessary briefly to relate the subsequent course of the Arnhem school conflict following my arrest on that decisive Sunday of February 8. Mr. Meyerink was sent to The Hague as a deputy for the board to demand that the Department of Education take the whole school matter out of the hands of the German authorities, since they had put the school into turmoil and were also arresting staff members left and right. He demanded secondly, that the Germans recognize the school board's dismissal of Veenstra; thirdly, that they restore complete control of the school to the board; and finally, that they immediately release the imprisoned board members, Boersma and Ploeger.

At the Department, Meyerink made a strong case for his position. As a result, sole responsibility for the Arnhem problem was assumed by the Department of Education. Mr. Noordyk, a Dutchman who worked in the German-controlled department, came to Arnhem as their representative and conferred with the school board. He condemned the attitude of Veenstra but appeared concerned that if he interfered, he would get the full weight of the party on his back. Noordyk had no backbone and was therefore not to be trusted. However, he did promise to seek a solution to the problems along the lines suggested by the board. But the promised solution did not materialize, and, tired of waiting, the board decided to take things into its own hands. It reopened the school without Veenstra, and all the students returned. Veenstra was barred from his classroom.

Two days later, the Department ordered the school closed again. An inspector and several officers prevented the classes from meeting. On March 18, a Mr. Van der Does was appointed by the Department in The Hague to take over leadership from the school board.

At seven different meeting places, almost all the parents of the Arnhem school students met, and they decided to form a unified front. They unanimously chose to keep their children home. Mr. Caspers, the headmaster, made arrangements to ensure that the children's education would continue though they remained at home.

When Commissioner Van der Does reopened the school on April 16 under the headship of Veenstra, only 30 out of 170 students showed up. None of the staff appeared, and they were immediately fired without salary.

The assimilation of the Christian school had thus been turned into a farce by the determination of the school board, the faculty, and the parents. A price had been paid, it is true, but the principle was worth the price. Commissioner Van der Does made one more attempt to reinstate Veenstra, but Caspers refused to compromise. He said that he did not want to work with Veenstra under any circumstances. Veenstra, he said, did not belong in a Christian school, or in any school, for that matter. When the offer was rejected in this way,

Van der Does threatened: "Then I'll leave you to the Germans!"

The students of the Van Loben Sels School were taught in small groups in their parents' homes. After school hours, the staff of the school was assisted by colleagues from other schools. Veenstra became a king without subjects. After a few days, he advised the parents of the few students still attending, to transfer their children to another school. He promised to support their request for transfer. Now all the students were gone. Veenstra, who had made such a sad, contemptible figure of himself, was appointed to be the inspector of elementary education for the province of Groningen. The Van Loben Sels School was closed, and on the first of August, 1941, dissolved.

Better no school than a Nazi school, the people of Arnhem believed. Better to receive no salary from the Nazi regime than to be its servant and supporter, said the teachers. Better to make great financial sacrifices in the fear of the Lord than to bend one's back under the yoke of the state. Better by far to get along with home tutoring than to sit in a beautiful school under the poisonous leadership of Nazidom. Better to suffer oppression and persecution while keeping children and conscience clean than to have them polluted by the evils of the enemy. Better to sit in jail and in concentration camps, having triumphed in the fight for the schools, than to be free but to have sacrificed both convictions and children.

In God's plan, the two imprisoned board members were released after eight weeks. And although I had to endure almost two years of agony, I never for a moment regretted the price. On the contrary, I thanked God that I was able to contribute in the spiritual battle against the Nazi menace. And I was also thankful to the board, the faculty, and the parents of the school for their determination. The Arnhem conflict had more than local significance: it had important consequences for all Christian education in the nation. As I said, Arnhem was the test case. It was there that the new Nazi order was to be introduced for the first time. It was in Arnhem that Leviathan first tried to sink his teeth into Christian education—and his teeth shattered. Those obstinate Christians are impossible to intimidate, the Nazis learned. They will not let themselves be assimilated. They will not bend. They can only stand or break.

School boards in the Netherlands took courage from the Arnhem struggle. Arnhem is the beginning of victory, it was said. We will all follow their example: better to lose all our schools and to have our teachers unemployed and our children at home than to let ourselves be tyranized by a power hostile to God. The early mistakes made at Arnhem were avoided and a strong stand was taken immediately; none of the rights of the school board or the parents were compromised. Many gestures of sympathy and thankfulness reached Arnhem from school boards all over the country. They had taken courage. By God's grace, it was owing to the conflict and conquest in Arnhem that the enemy failed to completely assimilate the Christian schools of the Netherlands.

If, besides the perversion that the Nazis could have wrought in the hearts of our children with their semblance of righteousness, we had been forced to nurture our children in the deceptive propaganda of the German Reich and Aryan superiority, instead of in the Holy Spirit of Christ and of God's Word, the yoke of the oppressor would have been unbearable. Therefore, in this respect, too, it was blessed to be persecuted and to suffer imprisonment for a good cause.

I drew immeasurable moral and spiritual strength from the fact that the day after my arrest the consistory expressed unanimous support for my entire sermon.

On the day that I was arrested, we were about to sit down for dinner when the feared and hated automobile carrying the sign "Polizei" drew up in front of the house. The three Gestapo agents who climbed out arrested me, searched me and demanded the sermon, which as usual I had written out in its entirety. I brought them the sermon. I could have gotten rid of it, but in this case I hadn't felt free to do so.

The week before, I had carefully discarded all other literature deemed illegal by the Nazis, but I did not want to do away with the sermon. I had spoken it in public. The sermon had been overheard and probably transcribed. This was an open, principial conflict in which no subterfuge or subtlety was necessary to save others. It was a consciously chosen conflict that had to be fought with spiritual weapons, at least on my part, for (it seemed to me) the Gestapo knew no spiritual weapons, only brute, stupid, vicious violence.

I was permitted to finish dinner with my family, but one agent stood guard while the other two searched my study, desk, and library. They emerged with a suitcase full of "suspicious" papers, letters, and books. They were especially incensed by tracts relating to our mission to the Jews in Arnhem, of which organization I was chairman at the time, and also by a collection of sermons by Rev. Niemoller. At the table I read Matthew 5:1-12 and prayed for my wife and child, for the congregation, and for the Gestapo men who had arrested me. Although parting with my wife and year-old child was painful, we were comforted by the Lord because it was for the sake of righteousness.

The police car carried us to the famous "Utrecht Road," the seat of Nazi-German (in)justice. The interrogation began immediately and lasted five hours to six p.m. The idea of an interrogation is to get the prisoner to talk as much as possible and, in this way, to collect as much incriminating material as possible. In the forefront of my mind during the ordeal, I kept the words of Jesus: "Behold, I send you out as sheep in the midst of wolves; so be wise as serpents and innocent as doves. Beware of men; for they will deliver you up to councils, and flog you in their synagogues, and you will be dragged before governors and kings for my sake, to bear testimony before them and the Gentiles. When they deliver you up, do not be anxious how you are to speak or what you are to say; for what you are to say will be given to you in that hour: for it is not you who speak, but the Spirit of your Father speaking through you" (Matt. 10:16-20).

This was the tension that pulled at me. On the one hand, I had to be "as wise as a serpent"—in other words, not aggravate my questioners needlessly, nor do or say anything foolish, while on the other hand, I had to be "as harmless as a dove"—that is, I must not muddy the situation nor cleverly avoid the issues in order to save myself. The latter is especially important with regard to spiritual issues. By way of final accounting, Christ also said: "So everyone who acknowledges me before men [not behind their backs, but to their faces], I will also acknowledge before my Father who is in heaven."

In the judgment of the Gestapo, my sermon was, of course, a "deutschfeindliche Hetze" (hostile and inflammatory diatribe against the German Reich). I tried to explain to my interrogators that they tended to view all phenomena, no matter what the field, in political categories—as either "deutschfeindlich" or "deutschfreundlich" (hostile or friendly toward the Germans). They saw everything through political spectacles. But art objects ought to be viewed through the spectacles of art, scientific matters through the spectacles of science, and matters of worship and of the church through spectacles peculiar to them.

The "No" of God's Word is directed at everyone who will not bow before God's Word, whether it be the German state, our own government, my own church, my wife, or myself. The preaching of the church is, after all, based on a divine authority; its prophetic critique extends everywhere, allowing no bomb shelters or sanctuaries to go untouched. This means that I could not exclude the occupying forces or National Socialism from the critique of God's Word. Just as the principles and practices of Christian political parties are subject to the Word of God, so too is every person.

Can Christ surrender His Kingship? I was therefore compelled to speak as I did. But these biblical truths were unfamiliar to my interrogators. They had been corrupted by the concept of state absolutism and by the idolatrous worship of the Third Reich.

After questioning me on my sermon for several hours, my interrogators broached the subject of Rev. Niemoeller, whose sermons lay on the table in front of us. "What do you think of Niemoeller?" they asked me. I began by observing that what I thought of my German colleague was not what was at issue. But I went on to say that, although I did not have a complete picture of the German church conflict because our sources of information were not reliable, I respected and loved anyone who for Christ's sake dared to say "No" to those in power. The fact that they had taken me prisoner simply and solely because the church wished to retain its identity and refused to betray the Gospel, was a fair indicator of the Gestapo's attitude toward the church, I concluded.

But I, of course, said my captors, spoke out of ignorance. Niemoeller was not in a concentration camp because he had preached God's Word, but because he was stubborn and stupid, and because, just like me, he had made politically inflammatory speeches from his pulpit under the pretense of preaching about the Sermon on the Mount.

I was also asked if I had made any contact with Mr. Caspers or with the imprisoned school board members, Boersma and Ploeger. That too was illegal. Having visited the wives of the imprisoned men was also held against me. First, my interrogators began by trying to instruct me in the role of the church, saying that I should preach the Gospel without commenting on affairs of state, but that I should confine my work to the welfare of souls and the comfort of the sick and needy. Then they told me that I could no longer visit the wives of imprisoned men in order to bring them comfort and counsel. This too was political propaganda. Because these Nazis were complete nihilists without conscience, it was impossible to talk with them and hold them to anything that they had said earlier. The morality of opportunism ruled. They would say first one thing and then another—anything that seemed necessary at a particular moment to reach their goal. They had no moral norms and no laws over them. As their captive, I was at the mercy of these persons from the underworld, subject to the whims of criminals and psychopaths ruled by demons.

There I stood before these perverted human beings, all of them united by a blind hatred for anything or anyone who dared to stand up against their system. Because the church, when it truly desires to be worthy of its name, embodies the most resolute principial resistance to any immoral system or world view, the Nazis directed their strongest hatred against the church, which, in their eyes was unjustifiably opposing their policies.

A convenient point of attack in my case was the fact that a short time before my arrest, my congregation and I had taken a collection in the church for our work among the Jews. My role in this appeared more seriously incriminating because I had been chairman of the committee directing this work. The Gestapo then painted for my benefit a repulsive picture of the Jews as individuals and as a race. I was asked if I really believed that there was even a single Jew on the face of the earth who would become a Christian convert out of honest motives. What would I do now, they continued, in view of the new light cast on the Jewish question by National Socialism, if a Jew did present himself for baptism? Did I understand that baptizing a Jew would constitute a public insult and offence to the new order?

My answer was this: "For me, only what Christ says and commands is conclusive. 'Preach the Gospel to all creatures,' He said—not, 'to all creatures except the Jews.' And Christ added, 'Beginning in Jerusalem,' the center of Judaism. 'And he who believes and is baptized will be saved.' If the King of the Church says that he who believes must be baptized, who am I to say: 'Except the Jews'?

"Whether or not the Jews are more evil, more obnoxious, or of a lower race has nothing to do with it. A man is not baptized as a sign and seal of his goodness and nobility. On the contrary, baptism is a sign and seal of man's sinfulness and unworthiness before God and is at the same time symbolic of the grace of Christ, whose blood cleanses us from all sin. The fact that baptism was instituted for all races, classes, and nations knocks each of us from his pedestal and reveals us as all equally guilty before God, so that we are all compelled to live out of the same grace."

Next, my interrogators brought up my prayer for the Queen as proof that I was partisan and an enemy of Germany. As early as 1941, secret bulletins went out to all kinds of National Socialist organizations, urging them to send spies to all church services in order to report which clergymen prayed for the royal family and for the government of the Netherlands. In the Arnhem association of ministers we had examined one of these bulletins and discussed the matter. We agreed that we must remain loyal. God's Word commands that "supplications and thanksgiving be made for all men, for kings and all who are in high positions, that we may lead a quiet and peaceable life, godly and respectful in every way" (I Tim. 2:1,2).

It seemed to me as the afternoon progressed that when my interrogators felt some stab of conscience or were at a loss for words, they quickly jumped to another topic. At least, this was the way the more decent ones reacted. I was blessed in this respect—others I had heard of would begin abusing the prisoner, cursing and raving at him. But I was never mistreated during my interrogation, though many thousands of others were subject to sadistic forms of torture by the upholders and defenders of the "right."

About six o'clock that Sunday evening, I was brought by automobile to the House of Detention.

At 8:30 Friday morning, February 13, I was again taken in for questioning. I was pressured to sign a statement that had been drawn up after my first interrogation. It was read aloud to me. Various passages from my sermon had been included. Some of the Gestapo's conclusions, including the charges against me, I totally rejected, for they were completely unfounded. I was told to confess that I had made inflammatory, anti-German statements and that I had misused the pulpit for political purposes.

When the statement was pushed under my nose for me to sign, I refused. Then the threats came fast and furious.

"We've got other means to make you confess. Until now we've treated you fair and square because we thought you were a decent man. But it turns out you're nothing but a common criminal! You know what Seyss Inquart (the National Socialist, Nazi commander of Holland) said? He said, 'He who is not for us is against us!' Anyone who is not for us will suffer the consequences. Have you ever heard of a concentration camp? That's where you can go and die. And you'd better not count on any sympathy either. Stupid fool, think of your wife and child! Don't make them victims of your insane stubbornness.

"Don't you know that the 'good old' days are gone? Those who can't or won't go along with us will be cleared out of the way. You like Niemoeller so well, but he's been in jail for years already. The same thing can happen to you, except that you won't become world-famous like your colleague. If you don't sign, we'll see to it that you end up in a concentration camp and that nobody ever hears of you again."

The spokesman closed with an S.S. theme borrowed from Nietzsche: "Don't in any way count on our mercy; we don't know the meaning of the word. With your weak constitution, you'll rot in a concentration camp! But that's not our affair. You have only yourself to blame." He ranted on like this for another quarter of an hour.

"You can keep at me like this for two weeks," I answered, "but it doesn't impress me in the least. One day you'll be called to account by God for what you do, and I too will be called to account for what I do. To the best of my knowledge, I have never yet signed anything contrary to God and my conscience, and I don't intend to do so now. You know my position. I preached as I preached not out of enmity toward Germany, not out of political considerations, but only out of obedience to Christ and His Word. Put that in your statement and say I'm guilty of that. Say I'm guilty because I would rather obey God than man, that I would rather serve

God than the National Socialist system. Put that down, and
then I'll sign."

Again, intimidation was hurled at me—new threats and old
ones, some shouted, some whispered cajolingly. Then I was
marched out of the room while they conferred on how to
break my resolution.

I was brought to one of the cells in the basement of the
building. It was freezing cold! The unheated cell with concrete floor in which I was installed was completely bare and
couldn't have been any larger than six feet by six feet. There I
was, locked up.

But it wasn't long before I heard signs of life from the cell
next door. Only a thin wall separated the two cells, so we
made contact quite easily. But one still had to be careful, even
in a Gestapo jail, for waiting rooms and cells were often
wired with eavesdropping devices to enable the Germans to
listen in on prisoners' conversations. My neighbor established
contact cautiously by whistling a hymn.

I was deeply moved by the melody and sang along quietly.
Then my neighbor waited, apparently to monitor my reaction. I tapped and said, "Thank you for the beautiful
melody. I know the words, and I'm happy to hear that even
under these conditions you're still willing to praise God. The
love of God is something they can never take away from us.
Do you believe that too?"

"Yes, I do," he answered. "It's our only source of strength
in this miserable situation."

"Who are you?" I asked.

"Schulte Nordholt from Zwolle. My brother's a prisoner
here too. But they'll never get anything out of us; we won't
talk. Who are you?"

"I'm Reverend Overduin from Arnhem."

"Then I know you. When I was a student in Kampen,you
preached and spoke to youth rallies there several times."

We then strengthened and comforted each other with the
Word of God for a wonderful hour. Schulte Nordholt
belonged to the underground and had been caught

distributing "illegal" literature. His interrogation had been much more severe than mine. He had been badly abused by the Nazis in their attempt to extract from him the names of other underground workers. He possessed a deep awareness that he could endure only in the power of Christ, not by his own power. After what I judged to be about one hour, I was again taken from my cell.

The German Gestapo officer said, "We've decided what to do. We'll stop at nothing, not even the worst, if you refuse to sign."

I had my answer ready: "You know my position. I'll stick to it." So the day passed: threat, refusal, to the cell, back again, until seven that evening.

When I was returned to my cell the second time, I heard muffled sobs coming from the next cell. I again asked who was next to me. This time it was a communist who had just been picked up. He had chronic stomach problems and was in sad shape. God gave me the opportunity to let him know that, although I was in the same predicament as he was, I was in good hands—I could even sing. I then told him about the sermon for which I had been arrested:" 'Blessed are you if you are persecuted.' Respectable pastor or communist—we all need Jesus to save us. That's where to look. It's the only place still open to you. Your wife can't help you. Your party can't help you. Only God is willing and able to help. All you have to do is pray. Would you like me to pray for you?" I waited.

"Yes, I'd like that," he answered.

And we prayed together, a communist and a Protestant pastor. God always gives work to His servants. No time is wholly lost. When Paul was imprisoned, he could proclaim: "But the Word of God is not bound." I could always bring that Word—to believers and unbelievers, to fellow prisoners and to Gestapo police. The results were left to Him, and He did with it as He saw fit.

At last, I had to appear before the Gestapo again. A section had been added to the statement prepared for me, which

pointed out all the passages and inferences to which I had ob-
jected and which I had refused to sign. In this form I signed
the statement. One might ask if it weren't just stubbornness
to refuse to sign. It is very difficult to calculate what is practical and wise in the face of authorities ruled by expediency,
especially as every supervisor of the Gestapo reacted differently.

On another level, my moral victory was probably a set-
back, for it surely added to my sentence. What good did it do
for me to protest against the political vision of the Gestapo in
a spiritual conflict between the church and the Christian
school on one side and National Socialism on the other. The
statement sent to the Gestapo headquarters in The Hague was
accompanied by notes and advice regarding the guilty person.
However, I never regretted the stand I took, not even later,
when I experienced the fearful consequences of colliding with
the Gestapo.

In Prison

To step from freedom into a prison cell is a strange sensation. It is interesting to observe in oneself the psychological changes that are a result of imprisonment. One enters a completely different world. Its sorrows and joys, its disappointments and surprises are different from life outside. The imprisoned person has to adjust to a life of total dependence and innumerable restrictions. Just as the gifts of breathing, walking, eating, and sleeping are often appreciated only when illness interferes with their normal functions, the privileges of freedom that we take for granted are really understood only in prison. In ordinary life, we do what we want to a certain extent, but in jail everything is prescribed. Most things are forbidden, and permission, which is required to do anything, is seldom granted.

The days and nights pass slowly, leaving the prisoner in a small cell with very little light. He can't even see outside, for the single window is too high to reach, and its pane is smoked glass.

The first item on the new prisoner's agenda must be a swift adjustment from the pace of free life to that of prison life. Those with slow or weak powers of adjustment have a very

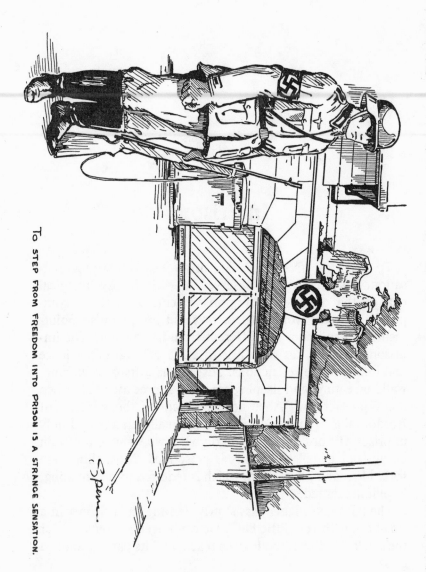

TO STEP FROM FREEDOM INTO PRISON IS A STRANGE SENSATION.

difficult time in prison. Their hearts and stomachs, their thoughts and dreams cling to the life of freedom; they do nothing but compare the misery of the present with the joys of the past. Eventually they drown.

They feel sorry for themselves, and they are constantly preoccupied with their own problems. Therefore, they are not able to realize that they themselves and their circumstances are not the most important things in the world. They are unable to open their eyes to the reality of God's plan, which is much more important and much more glorious than the world of personal concerns and desires.

After I had been taken to the House of Detention on Sunday evening, February 8, and the Gestapo had delivered me to the director to enter my name in the register (generally regarded as an honor roll in those days), I received a warm welcome from the director and some of the jailers. We had previously become acquainted through some of my visits to prisoners and the religious services I had conducted in the prison from time to time. I had also been in the habit of delivering packages to the political prisoners two or three times a week.

Only a few weeks earlier, I had preached on the text: "Cast all your anxieties on him, for he cares about you" (I Peter 5:7). My audience at that time had included Rev. Van Raalte (whom I would meet again in Dachau), Mr. Versluys, a teacher at the Christian high school, and Mr. Caspers, the headmaster. At the time, I told them: "The distance between us is not all that great, my friends." They were sitting in small individual cells in the church sanctuary at the time, while I had stood on the podium, a free man. Now, a few weeks later, it had become clear just how small a distance it was.

Every time a new political prisoner was locked up, the prison staff, except for a few Nazi sympathizers, was thrown into despair. "Don't take everything so tragically," I counselled them. "We're here for a good cause—it's worth sacrifices. We don't have to be ashamed!" I added: "Two faculties will keep us spiritually fit and resilient, especially in prison. The first is faith, and the second is a sense of humor. Faith and humor. If we have these two things, then in half an hour we will be almost at home in here."

I talk about the power of faith all through this account, but right now I want to discuss the power of humor. It has been said that humor makes life milder and easier. The gift of a sense of humor is an extraordinary blessing. For those people who lack one, everything seems serious. They appear to the rest of us to act as if they, and they alone, carry the full load of human responsibility.

Humor acts like a block and tackle: it can make the burden of life ten times easier to lift. Even when one finds himself in what seems to be the midst of all life's troubles, a sense of humor enables one to enjoy the remarkable ironies and absurdities of life. Life is pungent and full of spice, even in a prison. Understand me well. Life in prison is wretched and terrible—but a sense of humor can help ease the tension. A person whose emotions have been used up in agonizing cannot cope with the problems of prison life. To those who think and live only in straight lines, all that I have said probably seems contradictory. It takes flexibility of spirit to see it.

Despite all the misery that I have seen, often I have been unable to avoid bursting out into laughter. Yet, it has always been saddening when my fellow prisoners would look questionably at me as if asking, "What can you as a Christian find to laugh about here?"

It is a good thing, I think, that many people do possess a gift for enjoying humor, and that they don't see the difficulties and disappointments of life only as tragedies calling for tears, but also as comedies with their lighter aspects. Once from Dachau, where life was horrible, I penned this to my wife: "In the beginning I wrote you that two faculties have kept me going—humor and faith. But there are circumstances in which humor dies. Fortunately, faith doesn't die along with it; instead, it becomes stronger than ever." Yes, there does come a time when humor is unthinkable. Events occur that are too barbaric and demonic even for irony.

At first I was disappointed that I hadn't been put in a larger cell, one where ten to fifteen prisoners lived together. This was denied me on the strictest orders, for I was to be kept isolated, another indication of my interrogators' attitude toward me. I was disappointed that I was unable to attend to my fellow prisoners. I would have loved to talk with them about the richness of God's Word and the indispensability of Christ. I would have rejoiced to give guidance to those without a foothold and without a compass.

Such disappointment cannot last long, however, in the presence of Christian faith. He who knows himself to be wholly under the direction of the heavenly Father is convinced that He has planned everything and that He directs it to a good end. God worked out His purpose through my being kept alone in a cell. In this too, I had to say, "No moment in this cell will be meaningless, purposeless, or worthless. It must produce dividends; all of it is part of the total plan of God for our lives, and it serves the coming of God's Kingdom." As I saw it, God had two purposes in mind: first, after a period of extremely hard work and high tension, it was good that I should once again find myself in quiet and solitude; second, I could focus on my contacts with the guards.

Not just prisoners, but guards, too, have spiritual needs. I had many opportunities to talk with them about the meaning of Christ for man's life. During my stint in solitary confinement, I never experienced any acute loneliness. Every morning we were awakened at 6 a.m. We had to wash quickly, dress, and put our dirty water and the reeking slop pail outside the cell. Then we were brought a slice of bread and a jug of "coffee."

After breakfast, I made the bed, and swept and mopped my cell. By then it was 7:30. Then I held an hour of devotions, as I did after every meal. I read from God's Word (Jeremiah especially braced me), prayed, and sang psalms and hymns. I did much singing. I would begin with the first Psalm and keep on singing—every single verse. Many of the psalms and hymns provided me comfort and strength. Psalm 3,4,6,9, and 13 are examples. The rest of the day I passed in reading, working puzzles, and talking with any guards who stopped by.

I was allowed no visitors. During the twenty months that I spent in Arnhem, I was never allowed to see my wife or child or anybody else. Only during the first four weeks I spent there did I get visitors, and these were the regents of the House of Detention; Rev. Talens, the prison chaplain; and Mr. B. Nyenhuis, a former catechism student of mine, who managed to pay me a clandestine visit every day.

I would be extremely remiss if I did not pay special tribute to my colleague, Rev. Talens. He did a great deal for the prisoners. Despite all the regulations, threats and dangers, he visited us almost every day with a bag full of forbidden letters and packages. He was one of the channels to the free world and to the "underground." However, the Gestapo had an eye on him, and he finally had to pay for his good work. Two days before I was moved from Amersfoort to Dachau, Rev. Talens was himself imprisoned. His age and health made me fear the worst for him. Later, he did come down with a serious illness, but God spared him, and he lived to see home again.

Mr. B. Nyenhuis was also a faithful visitor. He smuggled all kinds of useful things into the prison. Every day he delivered secret notes and kept my wife posted on my condition, so I never really lacked anything in Arnhem prison. This was also due in large part to the prison doctor, Mr. Mink. As much as he could, this kindly man prescribed special diets designed to strengthen sick prisoners. In this way, I received a decent ration of bread, butter, and milk. And in the afternoon, instead of regular prison fare, I had potatoes, meat, and vegetables with delicious gravy. Survival was no problem under such conditions.

Because my cell was close to the central heating plant, I never suffered from the cold either. The prison dentist, Berkenbos-Berends, who became my good friend, called me in for treatment several times, although at the time I had no need of dental work at all. In this way, he gave the prisoners a chance to leave their cells for half an hour and maintain some contact with the outside. Most prison guards were able and conscientious. Their work was sometimes dangerous.

After I had been in prison a few days, a guard put me in touch with one of my colleagues from another town, Rev. J. De Geus. He was in a large cell upstairs with twelve other prisoners. I was eager to get to know him. First we wrote notes to each other, which were delivered secretly by the guards. Then some of the guards arranged our exercise schedule in such a way that De Geus and I would pass through the corridor to the exercise yard at the same time.

The courtyard where we exercised was divided into six smaller ones separated from each other by high walls. Only one prisoner at a time was allowed in each cubicle to pace along the walls of the small enclosure for fifteen minutes to half an hour. The cubicles resembled animal cages, except that animals have bars to look through. The prisoner had only walls, except directly overhead where he could look through a grid to the sky beyond. The guards gave Rev. De Geus and me adjoining cubicles and then "forgot" to close the door between them. Soon we stood side by side talking.

About three weeks later Rev. De Geus joined me in my cell. Rev. Bavinck from Kampen had been arrested and was put in the same cell as De Geus. With Rev. Bavinck to take his place and assume his work, De Geus felt free to honor me with his unforgettable companionship. We began to make things as tolerable as possible. We smuggled more and more books and other comforts into the cell. Soon we even had a pretty little table cloth on our table.

Our wives made repeated attempts to visit us, but they were denied. This was difficult to accept. It was especially hard because I had a child at home. To miss seeing your own little child grow up is to miss one of the great joys of life. When you are home, you notice something new every day. My little girl was only a year and a half old when I was arrested. How

I yearned for the day when my wife and I could once again hold our little girl between us. But this, too, we had to put in God's hands. Imprisonment is severe punishment—even if your treatment is excellent, and even if you are allowed to read whatever you want. The fact that you have been torn from your family and must live alone, divorced from your wife and children, separated from your friends and your work is a distressing trial.

On February 22, 1942, Dr. H.L. Both, a colleague from Arnhem, preached on John 12:32, 33: "And I, when I am lifted up from the earth, will draw all men to myself. He said this to show by what death he was to die." This sermon on Christ's suffering made a deep impression on us. We responded by singing a hymn, the last two verses of which say:

> I love the Lord; with joyful heart I'll bear
> the burden He has set aside for me.
> His will and purpose are my joy and blessing;
> whate'er aggrieves Him also injures me.
>
> I love the Lord; He'll always be my guide
> and lead me even through my darkest hour.
> His blood will cleanse me and His life renew me,
> transforming pain to praises by His power.

When God's Spirit makes room in the heart for His Word, shedding light on the cross of imprisonment and on a dark future, then the heart is filled with an unbelievable joy, and a shout of praise arises in the soul! What the Scriptures say is true: when you are persecuted, you are blessed—not pitiable, but blessed! Back in my cell, I reflected on the sermon. And I sang again.

A letter smuggled to me in prison from one of my colleagues, Rev. J. Douma, still comes to mind when I recall this comforting truth. In it, he drew my attention to the first chapter of Paul's second letter to the church of Corinth, especially verses 3-11. The conditions dominant then (during the time that this letter was written) clearly demonstrate the power of faith and the indestructibility of God's Kingdom. Paul's life is in great danger. He expected to die at any time. Danger lurks everywhere. He can be struck down at any moment either by Jewish plotters or by his gentile enemies.

Although Paul is in constant danger, however, and sometimes in danger of death, he doesn't try to arouse sympathy in the church of Corinth by complaining. He begins by glorifying God. Threatened by death, he moves from self-interest to God's interest and His Kingdom. Paul opens thus: "Blessed be the God and Father of our Lord Jesus Christ, the Father of mercies and God of all comfort."

Our crosses, our sufferings, and our dangers must be drawn up into another plan, namely, the plan that glorifies God. This happens not through our complaints, but through our praises—by our giving praise to the God who is called the God and Father of our Lord Jesus Christ. These names open up a world of grace and unassailable glory. "The Father of mercies." He is the source of all the mercies that we will ever need to ease our afflictions. "The God of all comfort." I meditated: I can be struck by no affliction so great that God doesn't have enough comfort to equal it. No matter what happens, I need never stand alone, helpless, uncomforted and without recourse; for He is the "God of all comfort."

Paul continues as follows: "Who comforts us in all our affliction, so that we may be able to comfort those who are in any affliction, with the comfort with which we ourselves are comforted by God." Here again he puts the comfort that we, in our affliction, receive from God into the service of the church. The living stream of God's Kingdom never ends in the sediment of individual experience as an end in itself. Every experience becomes a means by which we may serve and help others. We have a tendency to fluctuate from one extreme to another. Some of us speak about personal spiritual experiences in a wrong way, a way that is dangerous; for it makes the person who has had the experience appear very important, even central. Rather than the God who is the source of our experiences, it is the person who does the experiencing who becomes the center of attention.

In this way, we stand in front of Christ, blocking the way to Him who is worthy of all praise for what God does in man. In reaction to this sin, which gives an idolatrous place to experience and to the senses, others go to the opposite extreme of rejecting all discussion of experience whatsoever. No matter how dangerous subjectivism and personalism in religion may be, objectivism and collectivism are no less wrong; for in the latter we boast of God's work *for* us and the world but not of God's transforming work *in* us. Paul doesn't hesitate to tell the church of Corinth what has happened to him and what he has experienced in his oppression.

In the same chapter II Corinthians 1, we read this: "For we do not want you to be ignorant, brethren, of the affliction we experienced in Asia; for we were so utterly, unbearably crushed that we despaired of life itself. Why, we felt that we had received the sentence of death; but that was to make us rely on God who raises the dead." There is no trace here of Paul's playing up his own importance or of pleading for sympathy because of his suffering. Neither does he fall into a cold objectivism that anxiously seeks to remain impersonal, stifling all personal experiences. He relates these experiences soberly and clearly, insofar as they serve to reflect the glory of God. Deadly dangers have beset him, and he believes that he is about to die. God has permitted his predicament, so that in his temptation and chastisement Paul may learn to put his trust in God, who raises the dead.

As I sat in prison facing the possibility of a concentration camp, reflecting on my weak health and on the mercilessness of the enemy, I could do but one thing: put my trust in that God—the God who could, in a manner of speaking, raise me from the dead. When we find ourselves threatened by death, our faith does not allow us to begin complaining and wailing, or become rebellious, but it prompts us to put our trust in the God who works miracles, and who can rescue us from the very grasp of death. When nothing else is left in which we can put our trust, when we are deserted by everyone, and even our loved ones and our influential friends abandon us, God in His almighty presence continues with us and remains faithful.

Later, when I was in the concentration camp at Dachau, after difficult and, humanly speaking, unbearable days, I repeated Paul's words almost nightly: "He delivered us from so deadly a peril, and He will deliver us; on Him we have set our hope that he will deliver us again." As I stood exhausted, more dead than alive, too tired to speak a word at roll call, I often remembered those words. I would take stock of myself— my lungs were still inhaling air, my heart was still beating—and then I would take courage from repeating the words of Paul, which are both praise and petition in one: "He will deliver us . . . ."

On the one hand, faith is very down-to-earth and realistic. It confirms that by all human calculations one's chance of survival in such a situation is zero, that there is no possibility of being freed. At the same time, however, it also knows that God is all-powerful to free us. Clinging to II Corinthians 1:10, I never lost the deep confidence that I would be rescued as through fire, that I would emerge alive and whole as through the eye of a needle. And God did rescue me at the very doorway of death, and He brought me back into the place of the living. All God's children have had similar experiences during their imprisonment, experiences that turned a time of horror into a time of glory that they would treasure forever.

To those who never again saw their loved ones, this thought can perhaps be of some comfort. For they may have had an unbearably bad time, but they also had an indescribably good time. The heaven of God's fellowship descended into the hell of man's abandonment. We are therefore able to shout, "Blessed be the God and Father of our Lord Jesus Christ, the Father of mercies and God of all comfort," not just in times of peace and wealth, but also in the hour when we face death. This was true in Arnhem prison, and it was also true in the depth of my soul during my life-and-death struggle in Dachau.

About once a month, usually on a Tuesday night, a hoarse German voice would bellow down the Arnhem prison corridor, calling the names of those who would be transported the next morning. This meant that those whose names had been called would be shipped to Scheveningen the next day. One Tuesday night, long after my incarceration, it was nearing 9 P.M. In our cell, De Geus and I listened to the Gestapo shout and intimidate. Some forty names were called out. Ours were not among them, and I was relieved. My friend, De Geus, however, was apprehensive. He had a premonition that at the last minute, early the next morning, our names might still be called. His suspicion turned out to be right.

Because I lived in Arnhem and had the support of my congregation, my transfer was not announced until fifteen minutes before our departure. Otherwise, the news could leak out, and many would come to the House of Detention to say their farewells, albeit from a distance. Precautions like this were taken so that such demonstrations could, as much as possible, be avoided. On Wednesday morning, March 4, after we had exercised and returned to our cell, the guard informed us that we had to be ready to leave in fifteen minutes. Quickly we gathered some of our things, but our books had to stay behind. A few guards tried to cheer us up by saying, "Now that your case is to be tried in Scheveningen, doubtless you'll soon be set free."

The prisoners were mustered in the prison hallway between twenty soldiers with weapons at the ready. The commandant briefed us. Anyone speaking even a single word to his neighbor, or anyone making the slightest move to escape would be shot dead without warning.

Then we were bustled out into two paddy wagons. We passed first through Arnhem, where now and then we spotted acquaintances along the street, and then along Utrecht Road to the railroad station. There, from a distance, we were able to flash quick goodbyes to a few people we knew. And then we were on the train leaving Arnhem. Where to? We had no idea. We did surmise that not all of us were going to the same place, for we had been divided into two groups—one large and one small. De Geus and myself, along with a few Jews and a doctor, comprised the small group. To Scheveningen or . . . to Amersfoort?

To Amersfoort

We were transported in a third-class coach that had been reserved especially for us. All we could think of was, would we transfer at Utrecht or would we remain sitting?

The first option meant that we were headed for the dreaded prison camp of Amersfoort, and the second meant Scheveningen. The Utrecht Station would end our uncertainty and apprehension. When we got to Utrecht, the larger group remained sitting. They were on the way to Scheveningen. The smaller group, which included Rev. De Geus and myself was ordered to detrain. We were held in a small room of the railroad station that was also being used by the Dutch Red Cross in case of accidents at the station. Among the Red Cross personnel was an old Catechism student of mine. I asked him to let my wife know as soon as possible that I was being moved to Amersfoort.

After waiting there for about an hour, we continued by train, and soon we arrived at Amersfoort. Since there were only six of us now, we were not given a separate coach. The other passengers in our car quickly ascertained where we were going. Several nurses from a hospital in Arnhem were also among the passengers; they recognized me from my hospital visits to ill members of my church. They told their fellow passengers of my plight and asked them whether they knew Psalm 42:5. Some didn't.

"Never mind," they said, "we'll sing and then you join in. It's a beautiful song to sing to prisoners when they leave the station to go to the detention camp." As the six of us detrained and stood on the platform with our guards, a group of people gathered around and sang this psalm:

> But the Lord will send deliverance,
> Care for me day in, day out.
> I will live by this assurance,
> Sing it with a joyful shout.
> Even in the night I'll sing,
> Sing because I wait for Him;
> And no matter what may ail me,
> My Deliverer will not fail me.

It was a scene that I'll not soon forget—one of the many unexpected favors of our heavenly Father. Bright sunlight momentarily broke through the black cloud that overshadowed us. Our guards, disconcerted, stopped and waited until the song was finished. Then we picked up our luggage and walked to the camp.

To walk through the gate of a concentration camp for the first time is a strange sensation. We had often heard of the atrocities that occurred in these death camps, but everything that we heard was shrouded in a cloud of obscurity. The visiting hours observed in prisons did not exist in the camps. Outsiders, therefore, had no idea what the camp looked like on the inside, or what took place there.

Moreover, those discharged from the camps were sworn to strictest secrecy under penalty of severe punishment. They were required to sign a document promising to discuss nothing of the camp—and this meant absolutely nothing. Whether a camp consisted of barracks or of other buildings, whether the prisoners had to work or not—these were forbidden topics. This was even more true of such questions as whether the prisoners suffered abuse or hunger, or how many were sick, and whether these people received adequate medical care, and how many died.

After passing through the main gate, we walked through woods for some distance before we arrived at the actual camp—surrounded by barbed wire. The area was not very large. It had one entrance, a gate made of barbed wire, which was flanked by a guardhouse. It was attended by a few S.S. men who recorded the movements of the prisoners who worked outside the barrier. Other S.S. men with machine guns sat in several watchtowers raised high above the camp on poles so they could strafe the entire camp if necessary. They kept a constant eye on what went on in the barracks.

The winter of 1941-1942 was very long and cold. Winter was still hanging on, even at the beginning of March, and the temperature was well below freezing. The snow, which was actually more ice than snow, was several inches deep. A cold north wind was blowing when we arrived. We stood at the gate with our luggage from 12:30 noon to 6:00 P.M. We were already being introduced to camp life.

Not far from us stood several prisoners who more nearly resembled scarecrows than men. They were standing *am Tor* for punishment. *Am Tor stehen* (literally: to stand by the gate) was the equivalent of standing in the corner for a child at school. Perhaps these men had been caught not working hard enough, or maybe they had gone to the toilet too often for a rest and had therefore been charged with sabotage. Or maybe they had been caught "organizing" something.

I would quickly learn the meaning of the word *organize* as it was used in camp. It was used hundreds of times a day. One *organized* potatoes, onions, shoes, clean clothes, and many other things. It meant appropriating something or getting something done, or often, simply stealing something. Every time an S.S. man passed the men standing *am Tor,* they had to snap to attention. Their military salute was often returned with punches, kicks, or a push into the barbed wire. We thus got a vivid picture of what awaited us inside. When there were no S.S. men about, the prisoners begged us for food. We came from jail, and in comparison to Amersfoort, jail was a land flowing with milk and honey. We had bread, butter, cheese, apples, and sugar with us. We succeeded in tossing a few things to them. They didn't even stop to wipe off the dirt. They bolted the apples, core and all. The entire scene struck us who were seeing it for the first time, as strange, unreal.

At the other end of the parade ground, some thirty men were busy chopping ice, loading it into wheel barrows and carting it away. Elsewhere, another group of men was cutting wood and digging up tree stumps. In yet another place, two prisoners carried sand in a box with four handles. Finally, about fifty prisoners came crawling across the parade ground side by side, each one carrying a tin can in which he put every bit of glass, paper, metal, wood, and every matchstick and dead leaf he came upon. This was a demonstration of the famous "deutsche Sauberkeit" (German purity).

The tempo of the work changed from moment to moment. Whenever the prisoners found themselves unwatched, they went into slow motion, walking step by step, taking a quarter of an hour or more to load a wheelbarrow. Sometimes everything came to a complete standstill; everyone remained motionless. As I discovered later, this was part of the ongoing battle with death. The prisoners were on a starvation diet. The more they were able to conserve their energy, the longer they would live. Instead of working with hands and feet, the idea was to work with eyes and ears to avoid getting caught—"babying yourself." To "baby yourself" was camp slang for conserving strength, expending as little energy as possible, in a word, shirking. But it had to be done in such a way as to go unnoticed.

I repeat, our first impression of the whole scene was very strange, almost spooky. At one moment everything looked like a slow-motion film, or it came to a complete standstill, as in a snapshot, and the next moment you heard the whisper,

"White mice!" and the film suddenly moved into top speed. Anyone seeing an S.S. man approaching hissed the warning, "White mice!" And as the word passed from man to man, everyone speeded up the pace. "Tempo, Tempo!" some guard would shout, or, "Auf geht's, los, los!" (Let's get going, hustle, hustle!) But the faster tempo didn't last any longer than was absolutely necessary, for every thinking prisoner had but one goal—to survive. So save your energy—make no unnecessary motions! These were the catch phrases of prison camp life.

After we had stood in the cold for several hours to become acclimatized and to gain some idea of camp life, we were taken to the writing room to surrender our personal possessions. This process was supervised by a Dutchman. How such a man, no matter how committed a Nazi he might have been, could stomach the injustice and degradation done his fellow countrymen even for a day, I cannot understand. But the multitude of victims that passed by him from every strata of society seemed to bother him very little. In the name of the struggle "for Christianity and against Bolshevism," all our Bibles and hymnals were confiscated. Those who dared to conceal a Bible on their person and were caught with it were harshly punished. So we surrendered our Bibles. We missed them sorely, but we rejoiced that we knew quite a few passages by heart.

After our personal possessions had been recorded, we were taken to the clothing room. We had to undress outside. Undressed, we stood in the freezing cold for an hour. I suppose it was to get us used to the Spartan discipline of the camp. We were then issued underwear and an old Dutch army uniform. The underwear was in such poor condition that you could hardly tell the top from the bottom. If you complained that the outfit was too large or small, you risked a beating. We looked grotesque! The best we could do was laugh it off. Then, on to Block I, where we were to be housed.

When I arrived in the spring of 1942, the camp was still small. Three barracks or blocks housed all the prisoners—two for the Dutch and one for the Russians. The latter were kept strictly segregated. By the gate was a barracks that contained the barber shop, a writing room, a shower room, and the infirmary. The infirmary was subdivided into several small rooms: a waiting room, a supply room, an examination room, and two larger rooms—one for those with contagious diseases and one for "ordinary" illnesses.

Across from the hospital stood a brick building, the kitchen, which was equipped with the latest equipment. Between the hospital and the kitchen, but off to one side, lay Blocks 1 and 2. Behind the kitchen lay the barracks of the Russians, Block number 3. The Russians were all small, of Mongolian extraction, and appeared to be very passive and resigned. They were made to suffer terribly, however, from hunger, cold, abuse, disease, and desolation. Indescribable filth, stench, and disease prevailed in the Russian Block. In 1941 they numbered about 300; at the beginning of 1942, only a few dozen remained. The rest had died a slow miserable death.

In May of 1942, the Russian Block was converted into a hospital. One dismal morning all the Russians—about fifty in all—including those who were sick, unable to walk, or dying, were ordered to fall in before their barracks. They were loaded into several trucks in order, they were told, to be transported to southern France for a period of recuperation. About noon, the trucks returned with the S.S. men drunk and boisterous, but without the Russian prisoners. The trip to southern France was finished. As souvenirs the soldiers brought back some of the Russians' clothing and shoes. Thus, those Russians who had not previously died from hunger and beatings during the fall and winter of 1941-1942 had been shot to provide the space for a camp hospital. For the Nazis, it was the simplest, most rational way to make space available. So this last handful of captive Russians met their end in some unknown field or forest at the hands of a group of drunken S.S. men.

Ironically, later in my imprisonment, several barracks were

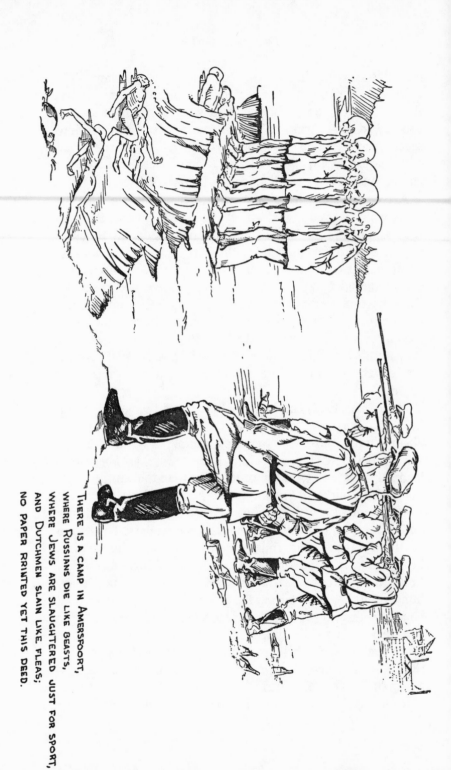

There is a camp in Amersfoort,
Where Russians die like beasts,
Where Jews are slaughtered just for sport,
And Dutchmen slain like fleas;
No paper printed yet this deed.

added to the camp. The newer ones were not made of wood like Blocks 1, 2, and 3. The total number of prisoners in the camp during my stay fluctuated between 600 and 1200. Amersfoort wasn't really a concentration camp, but a transit camp. It was used for short-term imprisonment, for those with light sentences or for those en route to camps in Germany. Almost every week, transports to Germany and elsewhere were being organized. At such times, everyone was mustered for roll call and the numbers of those to be transported were called out. Everyone dreaded to hear his number called. It was a great relief each time the danger had passed again—at least for another week.

After we had dressed in our old army uniforms and had been shaved bald, we were led to our new home and sleeping quarters in Block 1, Room 2. The place was a mess! A block was divided into four parts, each of which was a room. In the middle, was a narrow space with a few unfinished tables and a stove. This space was so narrow that one could barely get through. On either side were the cots—two or usually three high, covered with straw pallets for mattresses. In the roof were small windows for light and fresh air. The straw mattresses were too filthy to look at. Numerous ill prisoners had fouled them in every way conceivable, and most had at some time or other served as deathbeds. But these were minor inconveniences, for there were more serious things in store than sleeping on dirty mattresses.

Because of the ever-present dust, a block was a breeding ground for disease and infection. The 200 men who occupied a room, entered it with wooden shoes and several times a day. Three times a day the room was swept, which is to say, the dust was stirred up and spread over the beds.

Every newcomer received a metal bowl and a spoon. That was the extent of our equipment. Forks were unnecessary because solid foods were seldom served; everything was always thin and watery.

Once we were in our room, the chain of command at Amersfoort was explained to us. The camp commander was the supreme power; he commanded both the prison camp and the S.S. camp nearby. Next in command was the camp leader, who was the head of the prison camp. During my stay, this was Herr Berg, a predator who derived great pleasure from the agony of others. During roll call he loved to sneak about unnoticed behind the rows of men and catch someone in some violation, such as talking or not following orders properly. With a big grin, he would torment his victim.

Once he walked past the starving prisoners standing "am Tor" with a plate full of fresh herring, holding it under the prisoners' noses and asking them if they thought the fish looked delicious.

One evening after a heavy day of work, Berg added a couple of hours of penal exercises. They consisted of quick marching interspersed with "hinliegen and aufstehen," that is, we were made to march at a fast pace and then fall to the ground, scramble up, and march on again, over and over and over. It was an extremely effective way to reduce us to exhaustion in a short time, and a diabolically inspired way to rob the starved and weakened men of their last ounce of strength and to hurry them to their graves. That evening, as usual, another prisoner fell prey to Berg's punishment. After twenty minutes of "exercise," an elderly gentleman with a weak heart fell down and never got up again.

The block leaders were S.S. men who were something like sergeants, having command over a single barracks. Among them, too, there were several of vicious temper. I don't remember their names anymore, but I can still see their faces as they beat the prisoners, especially the Jews. Every prisoner was assigned to a work kommando, and each had its own kommando leader, who had to regulate the work of that kommando. Head of all work kommandos was the work leader. This was Herr Müller. He had a fat, sadistically sensual face, pierced by two bloodshot eyes. One of his favorite pastimes was to aim wicked, crippling kicks at the crotches of prisoners. His voice had lost all human qualities; he could emit only raucous barking sounds. We were deathly afraid to ask him anything, for he was so hard to understand that it was difficult to react quickly to his orders. This usually meant a cruel beating. From such treatment, one was expected to deduce what Herr Müller wanted.

There were other such bestial types among the camp personnel. They worked themselves into a rage almost every day and attacked their defenseless, weakened victims like demon-possessed men. When they had had their fill of groans and seen enough blood, they stood back, chuckling. These sadists tended to pick on the same prisoners, who for some reason caught their attention.

"Don't attract attention!" was one of the first rules for survival in the camp. Pity the man who was noticed by the S.S. for whatever reason. A prisoner might attract attention for being too tall or too short, for being clumsy or lazy, for being sloppy or slow to react. Once singled out, he would be tormented and abused until he expired—a victim to the brutality of the S.S. They were always out to get certain prisoners. These unfortunates continually drew extra punishment. Night after night, they stood "am Tor." They also drew the heaviest work kommandos, and they became the target of every Nazi inclined to violence.

Finally, there were the guards whose only duty was to see to it that no prisoners escaped. This was their only responsibility. The work, the tempo of the work, and such routine things were really none of their business. Many guards observed these limits and were indifferent to whether the prisoners were loafing. But many others wanted to accumulate good works, and they made it very hard for the prisoners, sometimes unbearably so. They couldn't stand to see a prisoner catch a moment of rest. Cursing and kicking, they drove the prisoners without reprieve. To them, the tempo was never fast enough, and every clumsiness called for a beating about the head.

Below the S.S. were the Prominents—prisoners who performed some function in the camp. Whoever succeeded in getting such a position had an excellent chance of surviving, for he could usually eat as much as he wanted. Moreover, he didn't have to perform any heavy labor, and, as a rule, he would escape the daily beatings. The camp elder was the highest Prominent. He was the link between the S.S. officers and the camp functionaries. Under him were the block elders or barracks leaders. Each of these had four room elders under him.

The room elder played an important role in the prisoner's life; often, he wasn't actually the oldest, but he was usually the oldest in terms of years of imprisonment. The survivors eventually got good jobs. Before Amersfoort existed as a camp, prisoners were kept at Schoorl. When Amersfoort was to be built and organized, the prisoners from Schoorl were used for this task. Later, Amersfoort veterans were used to set up Vught, another concentration camp in Holland. In Amersfoort the Prominents were usually communists or members of the O.D. (an underground police force organized to provide order upon the dissolution of German rule). In Dachau, they were almost exclusively communists, with an occasional social-democrat.

As a Prominent, one could do much good, but also considerable harm. Not all Prominents played an admirable role by any means. Some were just as bestial as the worst S.S. men. They beat and otherwise tormented their fellow prisoners—sometimes to death. In order to keep their privileged positions, they became willing instruments of their S.S. superiors. But among them were also many courageous and just persons who did much for their fellow prisoners and who saved many lives. Camp elder Van Putten, the top prisoner during my stay, was always available to everyone. He worked unflaggingly and without being partial or taking bribes to transfer the weak prisoners from heavy kommandos to easier ones.

Kommandos varied widely in the camp. You could end up in a kommando where there was no chance from early morning till nightfall to "baby yourself." You had to work at a constant backbreaking pace because the S.S. stood by,

A DEMONSTRATION OF THE FAMOUS GERMAN CLEANLINESS.

driving you on with words, with blows and kicks, or with clubs and whips. Whoever landed in such a kommando couldn't last very long, humanly speaking. But it was also possible to be assigned a job where there was little supervision or where the guard didn't care whether you worked or not, as long as you were moving when there was a check. It might also happen that one day would be very hard and next day easy, because the guards changed constantly and some were much more rigorous than others. All one's skill went into getting a decent work kommando or into getting out of a bad one. "Pray and work" made sense; it was a matter of life or death.

For this reason, I owe camp elder Van Putten a great deal. Upon my arrival, I was put on the Barbed-Wire Kommando, which had to take care of all kinds of heavy jobs, such as putting up barbed-wire barricades. But after three days, Van Putten managed to get me transferred to the potato-peeling shed. Van Putten would not be manipulated; he refused to be an instrument in the hands of Berg. And Berg hated him for it. Berg subjected him to increasingly vicious criticism and made life intolerable for him.

One night Berg appeared before us at roll call and self-righteously, as if he were the wronged party, denounced Van Putten as a fraud. Such a man, he said, was no longer worthy of being camp elder. So Van Putten was disgraced in full view of everyone and reduced to the rank of an ordinary prisoner. No one, however, believed Berg's charges. Berg merely wanted to replace Van Putten with someone who would harass and browbeat the prisoners.

A very powerful group in the concentration camp were the Sanitäters, those in charge of the infirmary and of treating the sick and ailing. In 1942, the infirmary was under the control of the two Bannings, father and son, both committed communists. But later, the son was executed, and the father was transferred to a German camp. Although the camp doctor was responsible for dispensing sick-notes, bed rest, and special-diet orders, these two men were able to do considerable good in their position as Sanitäters during their imprisonment. They were a couple of tough customers, but they were not out to give anyone a bad time. Several times they saw to it that I got clandestine sick-notes when I needed a rest to recover my strength. When I developed an infection in my hand from peeling potatoes, with the help of one of the doctors, they managed to drag out my convalescence to six weeks. One week would have been sufficient to heal my hand.

It was 7:00 P.M. in the camp—time for roll call. The room elder quickly instructed us how to conduct ourselves during the drill so that we would not be the cause of collective punishment resulting from a poor roll call. A bell sounded. The prisoners lined up, block by block. As newcomers, we were put in the back row so that our rawness and awkwardness would not be conspicuous. The block leader appeared with the camp elder and ordered: "Block 1, stillstand! Mütze ab, die Augen links!" (Attention! Caps off, eyes left!) Then the camp elder reported to the block leader how many prisoners were present. The block leaders in turn reported to Berg, the camp leader.

Roll call usually lasted an hour—an hour of utter frustration. It was never right. We weren't synchronized. Or one of the older prisoners was late. Sometimes the order "Hats off" had to be repeated dozens of times. Penal exercises often followed. The "guilty" were made to come forward, given a good beating, and then made to stand "am Tor." Frequently, roll calls were conducted in rain or storm, in extreme cold or intense heat. Had we been fed decently, this would have been tolerable, but these continual tests of strength and stamina were deliberately imposed on men who were seriously underfed and suffering from severe malnutrition. We were all becoming living cadavers. In three-months' time, for example, I lost 45 pounds, dropping from a weight of 165 to 120.

And I was living under exceptionally good conditions, for during those three months I was miraculously protected. I was never abused except for an occasional blow or kick, but that hardly counted. In Dachau, however, things would be different. A hellish time awaited me there. At least in Amersfoort we always got enough sleep. The day didn't start until about 7:00 A.M. Roll call was at 8:00. And at 7:00 or 7:30 in the evening, we could rest again—if no penal exercises had been imposed.

Since it was our first evening in Amersfoort, we had to be drilled in the military maneuvers of the camp; marching, rhythm, falling in quickly, holding a flawless roll call, etc. We were glad to get back to the barracks at 9:30 to eat a piece of bread. We had been made to assimilate quite a lot that day. It was hard to believe that we had eaten breakfast in Arnhem that same morning, unaware of what awaited us in Amersfoort. It seemed like hundreds of hours ago.

Ministry in the Concentration Camp

From the beginning of my imprisonment, I clung to the idea that God rules over everything, even over the evil and injustice done by man. God was fulfilling His plan for my life even during the height of the S.S. atrocities. To see only the people who are the cause of your anguish is to see only the superficial; then you cannot accept your suffering. You become angry, rebellious, and bitter, or out of self-preservation and deliberate calculation, you accommodate yourself as best you can and resign yourself to the inevitable.

But life is so much richer when we allow God to free us from our negativity and to place us in the light of His all-wise will. Thank God that I was able to view my arrival in Amersfoort in a positive way. This is not to say I ignored the fact that I might perish in this valley of death and never return, but I could not let such considerations rule my life, for then I would be overcome by them. What I had to face, ultimately, was not just future possibilities, but a present reality. This real present included the fact that God had allowed me to be brought to Amersfoort. He must have had a wise and merciful purpose in mind. He must have wanted to use me there as His minister.

It is a mistake to think that God can be served only through the conventional callings such as preaching, visiting the sick, family visiting, catechetical instruction, evangelism, youth work, and social work when we are free. God also wants to use us as his servants when we are imprisoned. In many respects, it provides an opportunity for an even richer kind of service. The prison chaplaincy is, of course, a fine institution, but there is always a gulf between the prisoners and the preacher. Their experiences are different. The preacher is not agitated by the same needs as the prisoners, for he will soon go back to his wife and family, whereas the prisoners will remain in their cells.

But God works in His own ways. Pastoral work was absolutely forbidden in the concentration camp, and no clergymen were ever admitted to do such work. God, however, saw that the camp was full of persons in great need. Therefore, a few pastors had to be taken prisoner and transported to the camps. As prisoners, they could carry on their ministry even more effectively than as free men.

To be chosen by God and to be qualified for such a task is an honor for which one should be thankful. As disciples of Christ, didn't we promise, "Lord, I will follow You, no matter where You may lead"? And if the footsteps of Jesus Christ go straight into a concentration camp, can one then refuse to follow? Naturally, the flesh is hardly eager to do so. But when one has been given a shepherd's heart, can one refuse to be thankful for such a calling?

God made this very clear to me. As a result, every day was rich with unexpected experiences. My three months in Amersfoort was one of the most joyous times of my life as a minister. Never have I experienced such overwhelming blessings upon my work. When we are wholly attuned and devoted to the service of God's Kingdom, when every fiber of our existence strains to that end, then possibilities and opportunities for the advancement of God's Kingdom will show themselves, then we will always find people thirsting for spiritual conversation, hungering for fellowship with God, and asking to be shown the Way back to Him.

This was apparent to me even on the first day at Amersfoort. At 8 o'clock every morning the newcomers were assigned to one of several work kommandos. The work day lasted from 8 A.M. to 12 noon and from 1 P.M. to 6 P.M.—nine hours a day. But added to that were the one or two strenuous hours of roll call and exercise.

I was assigned to the Barbed-Wire Kommando, formed to build barbed-wire fences. Actually, our squad of twenty or thirty men went out with picks and shovels and wheelbarrows to chop loose the frozen snow and wheel it to a large hole—heavy work for someone not used to physical labor. Undeveloped muscles were subjected to violent strain.

This is not necessarily bad for a person. The body becomes accustomed to it, and a little pain never killed anyone. However, we were not fed in proportion to the physical output demanded of us, so our bodies wasted away like snow in the sun. This was the most inhuman aspect of the concentration camp system. Consequently, very quickly we learned to shirk as much as possible—to baby ourselves.

Every hour we had to switch chores from pick to shovel to wheelbarrow. We always tried to work in small groups so that we would get to know each other. Our kommandos included several cadets from a seaman's school, an Indonesian captain, a few army officers, and a number of civilians who had been imprisoned for being members of the O.D. Within half an hour we were immersed in spiritual questions concerning faith, prayer, and the person of Christ. In this way, the morning passed quickly.

Nevertheless, at noon we were happy to get an hour's rest and something to eat. Back in our block, we had to line up with our bowls to get our small ration of soup. It was an ugly sight and a fearful racket; a couple hundred men were milling around together, each "afraid his ration would be less than that of his neighbor." Jealously, each one eyed the ration of his comrade, who seemingly had fared a little better than himself. If ever anyone was bumped in the melee, curses would explode across the room.

A fight could break out over a place on the stove. In an attempt to get a few extra calories, some men would try to preheat their bowls on the stove. Acutely aware that all of us were short several hundred calories per day, each man searched for as many ways as possible to supplement his diet. One way was with heat from the stove.

The weak certainly did not seem to be inheriting the earth here. Some of the men in our rooms were in very bad shape. We had the privilege of having among us a gang of about thirty men from the Amsterdam underworld, career criminals who had held up a distribution center and stolen thousands of ration cards to sell on the black market. Almost all of them had nicknames and spoke a slang that was comprehensible only to insiders of the clique.

A few of them soon devised a way to get double rations. Where they found them I don't know, but these enterprising fellows soon managed to get their hands on a second bowl each. They would get the first bowl filled at the beginning of the food line and then butt into the middle to get the second one filled. To get back into the middle of the line took much shoving, swearing, and punching, and precipitated many violent fights. These crooks received their double rations at the cost of others who could then not get their full share. Articles were also constantly being stolen from our rooms. If one turned one's back for a moment, something was sure to be missing.

Once, following a scanty supper that merely served to stimulate the appetite, I went to talk to the room elder. He wasn't a bad sort, rather easy to talk to. I asked him, "Tonight when all the men are together, is it all right if I talk to the whole room?" He finally gave me permission, as long as I didn't preach a sermon, for that was strictly forbidden. We were allowed to discuss only technical and "natural" topics in our free time. I promised him that I wouldn't preach, but that I would talk to them about "the art of living." The room elder therefore announced that comrade

Overduin would speak at 8:30, and he asked everyone to be present.

After we had again cleared ice that afternoon, and when the hour-long roll call was over and everyone had devoured his piece of bread and cupful of surrogate soup, I climbed up on the table. Most of the men were already lying on their cots, tired out; a few still sat on their straw pallets or on the benches. I addressed them as follows: "Friends, I've only been here a day and a night. I'm sure I can guess what you're thinking: 'Who does he think he is? He no sooner arrives than he's already going to tell us how it is.' To tell you the truth, this doesn't sit right with me either, to ask to speak to you so soon. It would be much better for someone to speak who has been here a long time—someone who has seniority. So there had better be a pretty good reason for me to bypass these fellows and ask for this heart-to-heart talk with you. I'll tell you the reason.

"Today I freed myself from the press and scramble of that mob in the mess hall, and I stood back to watch everyone from a distance. Seeing your disturbed faces, your wildly rolling eyes, your anxiety about being short a few crumbs, and the elbowing and kicking, I asked myself, 'Will I act like that too in a few weeks? Will hunger and misery, the struggle for existence, the desperate fight against death make me just another ragged wave in that turbulent human sea? Will I too trample underfoot all human values and ideals to save myself?'

"To tell you the truth, I don't trust myself. When it comes right down to it, we're all carved from the same wood. One person may be polished and varnished and the other be natural and unfinished, but underneath we're all the same wood. Before me stand all kinds of people: communists, Christians, laborites, black-market dealers, those who don't believe in anything, and church-goers. And here I stand: a dignified, respected Reverend. I ask myself, do any of us understand the art of living? Yes *living,* genuine *living,* does not just happen! If you think it's something that just happens, you're wrong. It's an art! Those who know the secret are rare.

"When I stood back today to watch the struggle for our bowls of soup, I thought: 'If we don't even know how to divide and share our bowls of soup, how can we know the art of living?' We condemn the government and the church for failing to avert war at the tremendously complex levels of life, but we ourselves make war over a bowl of soup! How little we see ourselves as we are! We are critical of our neighbor, demanding the impossible from him; but we exempt ourselves from criticism, and we don't even demand all that is possible.

"Jesus spoke of the man who saw the sliver in the other man's eye and was unaware of the beam in his own. We're odd people! We congratulate ourselves and belittle others. But the church, that much-abused institution, says that exactly the opposite has to happen. That is, we must have enough insight into ourselves to become displeased and to detest ourselves, in the sense that we can't stand our own egotism and hypocrisy. Hypocrisy isn't a monopoly of church-goers, you know. The atheist too is hypocritical when he sounds off about brotherhood, solidarity, love for his neighbor, and the unity of mankind; but he doesn't even know how to share the soup in a concentration camp.

"There are those who think they know all about the art of living as long as they can go to the theatre dressed in the latest style. But as soon as these expensive pleasures are taken away, there's nothing left. What they *are* is not found in themselves! Their being is in their houses, their automobiles, their theatres, their clothes. Their conduct depends on these things. They are what they possess. If they have much, then they are much! If they have little, they too are little. If they have nothing, then they too *are* nothing.

"Such people haven't mastered life; they are at its mercy! For them, it is true that "clothes make the man" or "man is a product of his environment." Spiritually and morally, they are so poor that they can't understand the art of living. So you ask, what is this art of living, and who's going to teach us? I'll make the answer short: no one else but Jesus. If you think you can weather life in this camp perfectly well without Jesus, you're sadly mistaken. I'm not saying this just because as a preacher it's my job, but because you've already made it clear by the way you have behaved. And if *I* start living without Christ in this camp, then tomorrow I'll be acting like you too. And maybe even worse!

"And what does the Savior of the world have to say to us? A great deal, too much to tell at one time. But let me mention one saying: 'He who loves his life shall lose it.' If we in this room continue to carry on in the same fashion we did today, we will all lose our lives—precisely because each of us wants to preserve himself at the expense of the others. That way we'll turn our community here into a hell. Morally we'll be so sick that we won't have the integrity to rise above the misery of this camp. We'll sink and we'll sink deep.

"But Jesus has more to say. He continues, 'He who is willing to lose his life shall keep it.' If we deny ourselves, deny free reign to our egotism and put it to death, love and help one another, politely allow each other to go ahead in line (that soup isn't going to evaporate), and stop swiping each other's bread, then even in this external hell we will see the coming of a heaven of genuine concern and community, of real comradeship and self-sacrificing friendship.

"I know that everyone here who still has some conscience and a grain of humanity in him, will agree with these words of Jesus. But I know also, that, although everyone would like to see some changes here, each of us is too weak to start demanding sacrifices of himself first. Yes, I too! When it comes right down to it, I'm that weak too. God knows it better even than I. The Bible says, 'He knows our frame; he remembers that we are dust.' God therefore gave us a powerful weapon so that in spite of our frailty we may still stand strong! That weapon is prayer. Some of you may remember your childhood. When your mother put you to bed, first she prayed with you. Maybe she even made you pray for a 'new heart.' Later you thought, that's all for kids and old women. But now we see that it's the deepest wisdom and truth. What we need in order to understand the art of living is a new heart. Our feelings aren't right inside. Not with you and not with me. Before Jesus, we're all in the same boat. We're all sinners who need to be forgiven and who need a new heart, a genuine 'about face.' Then we will discover the art of living.

"Shall we together pray for that? And from now on, let's show some respect to those in this room who feel the need to pray before meals and before going to bed. By now I hope it has become clear to you that praying isn't as absurd as it may seem. It's the beginning of the true art of living!"

I then led in prayer, and everyone quietly went to bed. I felt I had made contact with the group as a whole and with each individual in it. During the next few days, whenever anyone got edgy or rough, he was told, "Hey, man, remember what the preacher said about the art of living?"

I never met Rev. Van den Bosch. When I arrived, he was already in the infirmary, seriously ill. He died a few weeks later. The camp was deeply moved by his death. True, prisoners died every day; but everyone knew Rev. Van den Bosch. He had earned the respect of the whole camp. Many touching stories were told of his labors, his clandestine sermons, his secret pastoral work, and his exemplary behavior. When I attended high school in Leiden, I used to go to hear him speak at mission or youth rallies. This noble Christian man had the privilege of finishing his rich ministry in the Amersfoort concentration camp. He had adopted the motto of John Calvin: *terar dum prosim,* "Let me wear out, as long as I am of service." In Amersfoort he had burned the candle of consecration at both ends, so it wasn't long before he was used up.

But God sees to it that wherever His servants are taken away, new ones arise to continue the work. The ministry of Rev. Van den Bosch had already opened many doors. But in the opinion of the room elder, a committed communist, my speech had been a little "too religious." He warned me to be careful because among the prisoners were several stoolies who informed on their fellow prisoners in order to curry favor with the S.S., especially if someone made an unguarded political comment or uttered "religious propaganda."

One form of punishment for such statements was deportation to a German concentration camp where harsh treatment was intensified. A few Roman Catholic clergymen who had been caught secretly hearing confession had already been deported and had died there. We had to be careful, but we just couldn't keep silent, especially since I had already been asked to speak in the other rooms of Block 1 and also in Block 2 that coming Sunday. In fact, the first Sunday in Amersfoort, I spoke four or five times.

It wasn't long before Rev. De Geus and I had organized a small group of prisoners who felt the need for a short daily prayer meeting. It was passion week, so we agreed that every evening we would present a short meditation on the seven words from the cross. But checks became more frequent, and the danger increased. Titus Brandsma, a professor of the Roman Catholic University at Nijmegen, held a series of lectures on a well-known preacher, Father Brugman—a very worthwhile project! I also heard his lectures.

But as punishment for discussing a religious topic, this aging gentleman was put in a special work kommando. The S.S. was determined to put a halt to such teaching. Several other Christians were also singled out for punishment. If it didn't stop, the Nazis threatened, all speeches, even those on technical topics, would be forbidden. As a result, when I spoke I used the subterfuge of technical topics. One of my talks, for example, was titled "The Airplane." To tell the truth, I know as much about airplanes as rabbits do about radios. To make matters worse, among my listeners were a couple of K.L.M. pilots. It was a precarious situation, but I couldn't back down. The Gospel of Jesus Christ in this instance had to be brought by airplane.

I began by emphasizing that a great deal could be said on this topic. Hefty books have been written about airplanes, I told my audience. One could fill a library with books about the construction of airplanes, on different makes, different types of engines, and so on. I continued by saying that quite a few interesting books had also been written about different airplane flights and expeditions.

Pilots had also written some entertaining stories about their exciting adventures, the dangers, the tremendous joy when the destination is reached. I asked them to recall the suspense accompanying Lindbergh's flight across the Atlantic. Perhaps, I suggested, some other evening one of the pilots in our midst would be kind enough to tell the rest of us some of his interesting experiences.

Tonight, though, I want to discuss something else, I told them. Tonight I thought that together we might reflect on the deepest, the most fundamental reasons why the airplane can be both a blessing and a curse. In peacetime, the airplane serves mankind as normal transportation; it brings people to their destinations very quickly, reducing the distances significantly and creating ties between the ends of the earth. But in wartime, the airplane can be a curse, in the service of satan, as it brings death and destruction with its bombs, torpedos, and guns.

In this way, it didn't take me long to bring the discussion around to the problems of technology and ethics, culture and religion. Behind all appearances and powers, all gifts and goods, we discovered man and his sinful heart. We therefore looked for ways to ensure that technology would remain a blessing and not become a curse.

However, some people look for a guarantee in general circumstances, maintaining that man is a product of his circumstances. But this is forgetting that circumstances are in large part also made by man. I reminded my fellow-prisoners that the interaction of man with his circumstances is undeniable, but ultimately man has to face himself, and find in himself the heart as the center and source of life. We may not, deterministically, blame our environment for all our sins.

It is here, I continued, that progress must begin—social,

national, international, technical, or whatever. Jesus Christ demonstrated this again and again. Anyone who tries to find the source of life's blessing apart from a change of heart and mind, that is, apart from conversion through the Spirit of Christ, is just playing around with superficialities and is really concealing the true source of life's misery.

By thus landing my airplane on the runway of the Gospel, I had plenty of opportunity to make a concrete and personal call to conversion and to convince my fellow prisoners of the indispensability of Jesus as the only true Source of blessing. In this way, we were able to discuss several different topics in some of the barracks.

Dangers and tensions continued to increase, however. Rev. De Geus from the beginning preferred to speak exclusively in small groups. He and I, along with a group of other interested men, finally agreed that it would be better if I discontinued my open talks. A few outspoken enemies of Christianity and the church boasted that they would see all the clergymen in Amersfoort hanged because they were misleading people. They wouldn't rest, they said, until religion was eliminated from the camp.

Because this was a practical question regarding method, and not a question of principle, we decided that from now on we would meet only in small groups by our cots. The birth of the O.D. (*Orde Dienst* or Ministry of Order) also made this move necessary. The O.D. was organized in anticipation of the time when the Germans would be forced to retreat and there would be no one to take over the task of enforcing law and order. The O.D. had no intention of being an illegitimate action group; it wasn't organized to engage in sabotage or espionage. Its purpose was to create a temporary source of order to safeguard the citizenry in the eventual vacuum to be left by the Germans. Weapons and a military organization would be necessary to control an unstable situation.

All this was, of course, an abomination and a horrible insult to the Germans. First, what justification had anyone to hold the outrageous view that the Thousand Year Reich would go down in defeat? How dare anyone even raise the possibility that the master race would not triumph? The Reich had been inaugurated by Hitler himself, and "Germany was winning on all fronts." In addition, and here it was easy to see their point of view, how could they permit the existence of an organization that was collecting and hiding weapons? What guarantee did they have that these guns would be used only after the war was over, and not before? Many who had been officers in the Dutch armed forces joined the O.D. Among them were some fine men, men of great courage who were committed to their country and to its people—not just with words but with their very lives.

Those in Amersfoort who belonged to the O.D. were about seventy all together. With them was a small group who worked for the English intelligence, including two professors from Delft, Mekel and Schoemakers. The latter two men fully expected to be shot. Mekel, a faithful Catholic, and I talked and prayed together many times. I had the pleasure of sitting beside him for two weeks in the potato-peeling shed. Every day we were able to discuss all manner of fundamental questions.

He also told many fascinating stories about his travel experiences. There seemed to be few places in the world that he hadn't been. He had participated in several expeditions and was extremely knowledgeable in the field of anthropology. Altogether, he gave the impression of being a very alert, intelligent man, but at the same time he was also a person with a warm heart and an upright, childlike faith. He too had no fear of death: he had undertaken his work on behalf of his people in full awareness that prison could be the outcome.

Mr. Mekel accepted his situation in complete peace and surrender to the will of God. I can still see him with several others being led from the camp to the place of execution. We watched, trembling with outrage and torn with grief, but his farewell was cheerful, and he was smiling. He knew that this time his travels would take him to a much better country and that he was leaving his wife and children in good hands—in the hands of their Heavenly Father.

It was a time of great psychological pressure. I can't begin to describe how physically exhausted I was. Heavy labor during the day (at least, for the first few weeks), constantly being driven to do more, exasperating roll calls, ravenous hunger, and then, after work, busy every minute ministering to the many who were in mortal distress. Constantly talking, constantly giving comfort, constantly sharing and sympathizing in the most blatant injustice and the most bitter grief. Physically, I was deteriorating fast, but my spirit remained fresh and strong.

Then came the nerve-wracking, fear-filled time of the trial of the seventy O.D. men. The German prosecutors who would decide the life or death of our fellow prisoners took rooms in a hotel across from the Amersfoort railroad station. The accused were assigned to German lawyers to plead their case. This help hardly inspired confidence. A consultation with such a lawyer usually meant a disguised form of interrogation. Some prisoners put a certain amount of trust in their lawyers; others had no faith in them whatsoever. The lawyers probably differed a great deal from one another. I am not at all sure about the role that they played. All I can say is that most of us were far from comfortable with them.

But no one could complain that the trial proceeded too slowly. I'll never forget the night the first group returned to camp. The prosecution had demanded that they be shot, and they were in deep despair. A few had had their cases dropped because of a lack of evidence. These, of course, had high hopes that they could soon go home. This would have been the case under a rule of law. But these men, who were given no death sentences, or even prison sentences, because of insufficient evidence (according to the clear judgment of the court), still remained imprisoned in concentration camps for the rest of the war simply because they had been accused of belonging to the O.D. In effect, most of them *had* drawn a death sentence, one considerably more painful than execution; for most of them perished after a long period of suffering and hunger and exhaustion.

In Dachau there was even a class of prisoners called the *Vorbeugungshäftling,* that is, those imprisoned to prevent a possible crime. The Gestapo reasoned thus: "Mr. Jones has the kind of mentality that could eventually prompt him to deal on the black market, or to listen to forbidden broadcasts, or to tell jokes about Hitler, or to utter defeatist sentiments about the war, etc.; so in order to prevent this possible crime which would damage the well-knit fabric of society, we will put this man in a concentration camp."

There he could do no damage; and there, sooner or later, he would probably die, miserably, like the worst of criminals. But no great loss. Anyone who might listen to a forbidden broadcast is not worthy to look upon the bright sunlight of the German Reich. Serious-looking young men in S.S. uniforms defended this infamous procedure as the highest form of justice. It made you wonder whether you were asleep or dreaming, whether it was they who were crazy or you.

But to get back to our O.D. men. They returned late at night, drained by cross-examination, hungry and fatigued. They needed spiritual strengthening from the pastors and priests in the camp. We immediately divided the O.D. men into several small groups. Then we read God's Word with each group from a Bible that had been smuggled into the barracks. We comforted them by drawing their attention to the Conqueror of all injustice and of all satanic powers—Jesus Christ. And we prayed fervently together. It was amazing how God sustained these men. They had to surrender everything—wives and children, their own lives.

To be sure, there was a slight hope, for some even a strong hope, that after their defense was heard, the sentence would be much less severe than that demanded by the prosecution. But how would the defense go? The suspense was unrelenting: What would the final sentence be? Would a motion for clemency be entertained? Would it be granted? They were tossed back and forth between hope and fear. Generally, however, the accused men attained a state of rest.

Whenever anyone was threatened by doubt, whenever one of them became weak and confused about how to respond to the questions and cross-examination, we discussed his problem in a small group. He was given advice or adjured to say nothing except this or that, and never to mention anyone else!

We lived in this suspense for fourteen days. Night after night we wrestled alongside these brave men, beseeching God to send deliverance and, if things should turn out badly, to unite our wills with His and to strengthen our families. One evening we read the forty-seventh chapter of Thomas a Kempis' *The Imitation of Christ*. Afterward, the faces of all the men were suffused with joy, for they had been comforted by the words of Christ:

> My son, do not let the work that you have undertaken for My sake break your spirit, nor any hardships discourage you. Let My promise always be your strength and comfort; I can give you a boundless reward. You will not labor here for long, nor will sorrow always be your lot. Wait but a short while, and you will see a speedy end to your troubles. The time will come when all toil and trouble will cease; everything temporal is short-lived and of little consequence.
>
> Labor with all your might; work faithfully in My vineyard; I Myself will be your reward. Write, study, worship; be penitent, keep silence, and pray. Meet all your troubles like a man. Eternal life is worth all this and yet greater conflicts. Peace will come at a time known only to the Lord; it will not be day or night as we know it, but everlasting light, boundless glory, abiding peace, and sure rest. You will not say then, 'Who will free me from this mortal body?'; nor cry, 'Alas, how long is my exile!', for the power of death will be utterly broken, and full salvation assured. No anxiety will remain, but only blessed joy in the fair and lovely fellowship of the Saints.

This chapter from Thomas a Kempis lifted us out of the depth of our misery to the height of God's eternal deliverance. Did not You, O Lord, descend from heaven into the hell of our forsakenness and powerlessness? How puny our enemy seemed in the presence of that one Champion, Jesus

Christ, who overcame death and the devil! The countenance of death was transformed: "O death, where is your sting; O grave, where is your victory?" Death was then seen as life's servant, as the gateway to eternal light.

A death sentence did not seem terrible anymore, and many shared this attitude. Most of the prisoners, in the end, did hear the death sentence pronounced on them. These men were quickly ordered to be transferred. And although our farewells were solemn, and we were all deeply moved and saddened, we were also filled with a joy and thanksgiving that surpasses all understanding. Most of the seventy had long known Christ as their Savior. Some of them had, until now, lived on the periphery of Christianity and the church. Only now did they understand the glory of the Biblical faith. There were some who had had nothing to do with the Christian religion, and who had had little idea what it was all about. But in a few short weeks they were made ready for His kingdom. They were all people hungering and thirsting for the righteousness of God, and in childlike trust they surrendered themselves to the Son of God as their Savior.

What a spiritual victory! God did not call His servants to the concentration camp in Amersfoort for nothing. Like it or not, we had to accept our calling. And despite the danger, I never regretted it.

Special Protection

I worked in the Barbed-Wire Kommando about fourteen days. It was a relatively heavy kommando: clearing ice, digging, pushing a wheelbarrow, transporting mattresses and cots, and, during the last week, shoveling coal. The coal was piled more than three feet high in the coal shed. Our job was to move the coal to the far corner of the shed with big scoop shovels in order to make room for new shipments. The work assigned to the kommando was very demanding, but we had a good foreman who, whenever possible, allowed us to baby ourselves.

Moreover, we weren't always under the eyes of our S.S. taskmasters. To a large extent the heaviness of a kommando was determined by the tempo of the work. The Bush Kommando, for example, was much more strenuous and was therefore greatly feared; it meant doing heavy work all day at a fast tempo. Lagerführer Berg had a great fondness for clearing trees. Often he personally accompanied that squad. He was a despot, sarcastic and mean. If a starved and weakened prisoner didn't swing his axe with enough gusto or didn't haul away a stump with enough speed, Berg tore into him with a whip or a branch. Then he would chop for a few minutes to demonstrate how it was to be done. This pace, which he with his well-nourished body could maintain only for minutes, was what he relentlessly demanded day after day from starved, broken-down prisoners.

I worked in the Bush Kommando for a few days as "relief." One day, we were hauling extremely heavy tree trunks. Even with five men we had trouble getting one log onto our shoulders. The log would have been hard to lift even for five healthy men; for us, underfed as we were, it took a tremendous effort to get that huge trunk up.

Berg spied us and became furious. "What! Five men to lift one little tree!" He began cursing and scolding, saying that we were just too lazy to work, that all we could do was eat. He came running over and kicked the three men in the middle from underneath the log; this left one man in the back and myself at the front. How we managed to carry that log I'll never know! We were nauseated with the strain. But this is how we were forced to work for the rest of the day. Five of us would heave a log to our shoulders, and then the middle three men would step out from underneath as quickly as possible to avoid another beating. Anyone who fell down, unable to go on, was hammered back into shape.

Normally, an unconscious person is revived with water and smelling salts, and given time to rest; in the camp, he was revived with kicks and a pail of water thrown over him. And then it was right back to work. This process was repeated until a person's body finally refused to respond and it was impossible to rouse him again. Finally, he would find rest, sometimes in the hospital, but more often in a deeply longed-for death. The Bush Kommando claimed more victims than any other.

In a few weeks I had lost much of my strength. I thought to myself, "I'm not getting enough rest in my free time at night." I had to speak, pray with others, and hear many voluntary confessions from people who had run into dead ends in life—through broken marriages and other troubles, or because spiritually they could no longer see a way out. When I saw my strength was diminishing fast, I went to talk with the camp elder, Van Putten. I told him that if I continued as I was, I probably wouldn't last very long in Amersfoort, and that would be a shame in view of my ministry in the camp, to say nothing of my family and congregation.

He immediately understood and, sympathizing with my situation, offered suggestions on how to escape the Barbed-Wire Kommando. Without courage and even audacity, you can't last in a concentration camp. You cannot let your life be lived for you and you cannot merely accept the suffering of camp life as an inescapable fate—you've got to fight for your life! The very next day I succeeded in "organizing" a doctor's note. I did not report to the Barbed-Wire Kommando but slipped into the potato-peeling shed and found a seat. This Sit Kommando was checked almost every day by the S.S. and anyone found there without a doctor's note was put into a special penal kommando. But at check time I produced my note.

In the potato-peeling shed my body was able to recuperate somewhat, except for my back and fingers; for we sat on benches without back supports from 8 o'clock in the morning until 7 o'clock and sometimes even 10 o'clock at night. I worked in the shed for about three weeks. One bonus was that here we could talk to each other all day as we worked. I was able to contribute a lot, but I also received much. Many of the hostages from Amsterdam were here. They were mostly intellectuals and had extremely interesting things to relate about their various fields. There was Dr. Gunning, the retired rector of the Amsterdam Lyceum; he was a spiritual source of strength for many, an open letter for Christ, especially in his room in Block 2. There was Dr. Hellema, a professor at the Free University, who, to his credit, was hated by the S.S. officers of the camp. He too provided clandestine spiritual support to others.

It is with great respect and gratitude that I also remember the brilliant conversation of Dr. Jan Romein, a student of Prof. J. Huizinga, the famous historian. We shared many wonderful hours together. He gave comprehensive answers to my many questions on history, explaining in detail numerous subjects such as centralization and decentralization in the modern state. We spent many fascinating hours discussing historical materialism, communism, Abraham Kuyper and Groen van Prinsterer and their program. He in turn wanted to know more about church law, Swiss theology, and other topics.

Here, too, I was able to meet Prof. Mekel, whom I mentioned earlier. I was grateful for every day that I spent in the potato shed, for it enriched me and broadened my outlook. I also thanked and praised God when, a short time later, these men were released and their lives were spared.

Of course, sometimes we became dreadfully tired of those endless miles of potato peels; but at the same time we were very happy that we had to expend so little energy and that we also had a chance to conserve our inner strength. A danger that threatens everyone in such a camp is that all he can think about and talk about is hunger, fatigue, food, and sleep. There were those who had no other interests. They simply couldn't talk about anything else; for them, nothing else existed. They began to sink to a bestial level, severing all bonds with the past and with normal human life. After their release, many had great difficulty readjusting to the rich diversity of life. All relationships except those pertaining to animal existence had been dissolved for them.

It was extremely important for a prisoner to be aware of all these spiritual perils of camp life and to reflect on them. It was therefore also important to make those about to succumb to these temptations aware of them and to help them combat them. A physical, a psychological, a moral, and a spiritual hygiene had to be observed in even the smallest details of camp life. Everything that meant an unnecessary, senseless loss of energy had to be avoided if possible.

When I entered Amersfoort, I had with me fifteen top-quality cigars. Although I love to smoke, I told myself, "Leave those cigars alone; they're only to be used to help you stay alive." Under the circumstances, smoking was dangerous. The body requires energy to cleanse the nicotine from the blood. Under normal conditions, with decent nutrition, this energy is negligible. But under the conditions of camp life, it would have been wrong to make such demands on my constitution at the expense of my ministry.

Many times I have had to scold—in a Christian manner, of course—my fellow prisoners for treating their bodies stupidly, with little self-discipline and responsibility. To many, smoking was a passion, an obsession. They would put up a bigger fight over a cigarette butt than over a piece of bread.

But in the camp a cigar was priceless! All kinds of things could be "organized" with a cigar. You could buy back your life with it. My fifteen cigars helped me out of many a critical situation.

When I developed a nasty infection in my hand and arm from peeling potatoes, I lived under "sick law," as I called it, for about six weeks. How this was arranged, I have already described. But after six weeks I had to return to the laboring ranks. My healed condition was becoming too obvious. I was in danger of drawing the attention of the S.S. Occasionally, they would look at me suspiciously, as if to say, "Is that guy still walking around with that huge bandage on his hand!" Had they pulled off the bandage and discovered a healthy hand, healed four weeks earlier, it probably would have cost me my life. So I had to come up with something else.

Meanwhile, I had established good relations with some of the Prominents, that is, the leaders of the prisoners. Now and then I treated one of them to a good cigar, which intoxicated them so much that they were willing to do anything for me. This is the way I got into the *Stubedienst,* the Room Detail. Every room had a room elder and a few helpers to keep the room clean, to dish up the food, and to see to it that things ran smoothly. I served under room elder Jan Noordzy, and I owe him much. He didn't help me just for the sake of a cigar; he did so as a Christian.

Those were good times for me. He saw that I was very busy in my pastoral work and that I didn't have much strength left. Recurring malarial fevers and bronchitis were rapidly undermining my strength. I worked in that job until my transfer to Germany almost five weeks later. Noordzy saw to it that I did only the lighter work, while he and the others, who were in better health, did the heavier work—which, to be sure, was still very light in comparison to that of the other kommandos. I don't think I worked much more than an hour a day. I was put in charge of the "Gamellen," the large containers in which the soup was brought, helping to dish it up, cleaning the "Gamellen" afterward, and returning them to the kitchen. This was a great privilege, because the leftovers that stuck to the sides of the "Gamellen" provided a nice supplement to my rations.

Of course, I had to keep my eyes open all the time. Anyone caught loafing during working hours, no matter where it was, would be punished. An S.S. man could come storming into the barracks at any time, and then you had to be doing something. I was always ready for such visits. When the weather was bad, I climbed up onto the third level of one of the bunks with a basin of water and a rag. I sat or lay up there reading one of the books smuggled into the camp, but when the alarm was given, I would suddenly be busy scrubbing the ceiling beams of our block.

When the weather was warm, I sat outside in the sun with our large serving spoons, a container of wet sand and an old rag, so that if anyone came along I was scouring the spoons. One day as I sat basking in the sun, I let my mind drift for a moment and suddenly a large chunk of concrete landed right next to me, thrown by an S.S. man who had caught me dozing. Had it hit me in the head, it probably would have killed me. That's how the S.S. gave warnings.

During the day, I found the opportunity to sneak into the infirmary. Armed with a couple of pails of hot water, a mop, and a broom, I pretended I was there to clean the place, but I really came to visit the sick. Whenever "white mice" appeared, I was busy scrubbing floors. New dodges had to be dreamed up every day so that this ministry to sick prisoners could be carried out.

More clergymen began entering the camp, Roman Catholic priests as well as ministers from the two largest Reformed churches in Holland. In a period of about six weeks, almost a dozen clergymen were brought to the camp, so then the work could be further divided. We also met together periodically to discuss the task of the church after the war. How we longed for the unity of the church, for a strong, united response to the distress of the world! We even began drawing up guidelines for this postwar project. But this preparatory work was rudely interrupted when seven of us were transported to Germany.

One evening one of my friends, a man from Zeist with whom I had spoken often, asked to talk to me. We found a quiet spot where no one could overhear, because he wanted to ask for advice that might mean life or death for him. He belonged among the "heavies," those who were to be shot in the near future. He had made plans to escape, he told me. In his work kommando he had established a friendly relationship with an S.S. soldier, who had contacted his wife for him. Plans had been tentatively laid: some morning when the S.S. soldier had guard duty on the kommando, he would send my friend outside the camp by himself as though he had work to do there. His wife would be waiting with clothes and a bicycle; together they would head for Zeist and go underground there.

Now he wanted my advice on whether it was right for him to go on with his escape. Everything was at stake—not just for him, but also for the soldier. During a careless moment he had signed up for the S.S., but now he couldn't stomach the job. There was also much at stake for the other prisoners. Would the whole camp be punished for his escape? That was, after all, how the system worked. If one man stole something, everyone was punished for stealing; if one man in a kommando was lazy, then everyone was forced to work harder. If one man escaped, it would certainly be taken out on the whole camp. It was a difficult decision, but we decided that he should go through with it anyway. We met again the night before his planned escape and prayed that God would allow it to succeed. I was the only other prisoner who knew what was about to happen.

The next morning was one of extreme suspense for me. Everything went as usual. At 8 o'clock the kommandos left the camp. At 9 o'clock the prisoner from Zeist was to escape. By 9 o'clock I was a bundle of nerves. "If only the alarm isn't sounded right away! He's still too close; they'll nab him for sure," I thought. Then it was 10 o'clock . . . then 10:30. At 11 o'clock the alarm was sounded.

All kommandos were ordered to return to camp immediately at a fast march and to fall in for roll call. Meanwhile, motorcycles and cars were roaring out of the camp, followed by bicycle and foot patrols led by dogs. He had made it! He had already been gone for two hours and by now was well hidden. Berg and Blockführers were livid with rage.

The roll call lasted from 11 o'clock in the morning until 1:30 at night. "Hats off . . . hats on . . . eyes left . . . eyes right," without letup. Then they simply left us standing. We got nothing to eat. Most of us had eaten nothing since 7 P.M. the day before. Hungry, thirsty, exhausted and tormented, we were tantalized and baited hour after hour. At 12:30 that afternoon we thought it was over. But no, it became 2 o'clock, then 3 . . ., 4 . . ., 5 o'clock. And all the time we were standing at attention. Here and there prisoners pitched forward. They were not allowed to be taken to the infirmary.

Then came 7 . . ., 8 . . ., 9 . . ., 10 o'clock. Still standing. We were coming to the end of our endurance. Darkness came, and we grew bolder. We were so cold and so tired that we began to lean against each other. We became a huge tangle of pain and misery—a thousand men lying against one another but still standing. Then suddenly from the machine gun towers spotlights were turned on us and a voice barked, "Stand at attention or you'll all be shot!" And again we stood at attention. Again, more victims slumped to the ground.

On it went:11 . . . , 12 midnight . . . , 1 A.M. We had been standing for fourteen hours, and most of us hadn't eaten for thirty. Finally, at 1:30 A.M. came the order: "Into the blocks, march!" Before we were on our cots, it was almost 2:30. We were scheduled to get fish soup that day. It was the first and the last time. Although it was mostly water, it contained little bits of fish and lots of fishbones. Our portions were small, only about a pint. But there was a big scramble for those bones. At night we still lay chewing and grinding on the bones. Bones have a lot of food value; they contain calcium.

Such things are hard to forget. Two other events incensed me deeply. One was the well-advertised doctor's visit on Ascension Day, 1942. The hypocrisy of the system was particularly insufferable. On paper everything was in order. Medical care was provided, but don't ask how or of what quality. For those too weak to do hard labor, a medical excuse was available, but not before they were at least half dead. Every prisoner was weighed once a month, and his weight was recorded. Even if you lost thirty pounds a month or your weight dropped below a hundred pounds, however, it made no difference. You didn't get a bit more to eat. The important thing was to have everything neatly recorded; then they could report to the outside world that every prisoner was getting proper care. Their weight, for example, was being carefully checked every month. An outward appearance of decency and humanity had to be maintained.

This calculated malice and duplicity were also evident in the feeding of the prisoners. About once every three months we would be surprised to find thick soup with meat in our bowls. Delicious! But it didn't take long to figure out why. Important visitors were coming: officers of the *Wehrmacht*, a committee from the Red Cross or from some other agency. They were allowed to look everywhere. They could come into the kitchen and taste the delicious and nutritious soup that we were fed. It was all calculated to make them think that the rumors of atrocities and starvation and heavy labor were just slander. On those days no one was beaten or driven at work. Even the bullies seemed to be impressed by their own magnanimity. They seemed somewhat self-alienated, hardly recognizing themselves.

A few days before the announced doctor's visit, we couldn't believe our eyes. The camp doctor gave a medical excuse to almost everybody. Not just to the many suffering from dysentery, not just to the walking skeletons, but to everyone with the slightest cold or headache. In no time at all, there were more people in bed than outside working. We didn't trust this sudden spurt of humanitarian concern. There had to be something else behind it. We soon found out.

It was Ascension Day. Every sign indicated that this was not going to be a good day for us—except for those lying in the barracks. At 5 o'clock, all the healthy prisoners had to fall in and undress on the parade ground. A staff of S.S. doctors was coming to check our health. A cold, vicious wind was blowing from the north. We stood shivering in the intense cold. We were left that way for three hours before the "helpers of humanity" arrived. They were having a good time with the commandant, and Berg seemed full of jokes. Those took another half hour. Then we were made to march past the ten doctors, who glanced at us every now and then. That was our checkup, the medical care which we all urgently needed.

These doctors, too, had been poisoned by Nazi ideology. Even this group of men, whom we had expected to retain their humanity so that they could see their enemies and prisoners first of all as people, were no longer real doctors or even human beings. The devilish cancer of National Socialism ate into everything and everybody, even into the hearts of medical doctors. The culmination of their visit, it seems, was a drinking party with the camp officers.

Since we are discussing medical care, this is a good place to mention Dr. Nieuwenhuis, our camp doctor in 1941 and 1942. He was a dedicated sadist. He preferred to treat his patients with a club rather than with a stethoscope. He caused many deaths. A few weeks after my arrival in Amersfoort, he was replaced by someone else. His successor was more humane. But a week after his arrival, too many prisoners were lining up in front of the infirmary for medical help. This infuriated the camp administration. The new doctor hadn't yet caught on to what medical "care" really meant in a concentration camp.

The commandant hollered, "It looks like a sanatorium around here instead of a work camp!" The doctors were expected to treat their patients in such a way that they preferred to drag their ailing bodies to work rather than fall into medical hands. You had to feel deathly sick before you would entrust yourself to a man like Dr. Nieuwenhuis. Although his successor, Dr. Klomp, was hardly Hippocrates, I never saw him abusing any of his patients. At first he didn't chase off enough of the sick, and he handed out too many sick-notes. But three or four days after his arrival, the commandant came to sit in during office hours to teach the doctor how patients were to be treated at Amersfoort.

The doctors who were imprisoned in the camp did what they could to help. They were not assigned to any of the work kommandos, but they helped an endless line of men with wounds, sores, and infections. Because they lacked even the most elementary instruments, they had to resort to crude remedies. Boils, for example, were treated in a very primitive and painful way. A knitting needle was heated red hot in the stove and jabbed into the heart of the boil. It seemed to be very effective, though crude.

Another unforgettable incident occurred on what we called our "mattress night." I relate this merely as a sample of the many indignities that we were subjected to, for every day brought new, painful surprises. The normal order of things was bad enough, but the camp administration was ingenious in devising something new for us each day. Berg had a fecund and macabre imagination. Whenever he came walking onto the parade ground with his ominous smile, we knew that he was gleefully anticipating the mischief that he was about to inflict on us.

One night he gave us a lecture attacking all the black market dealing going on in the camp. According to him, there were fabulous amounts of money, onions, potatoes, and carrots stashed away in our straw mattresses, as well as a treasury of gold rings, watches, and jewelry. Therefore, Berg gave orders for all mattresses to be brought from the barracks and stacked on the parade square in one huge pile. It had been raining continuously for several days, so the square was one gigantic mud hole. Although we were already extremely tired, we had to drag out more than a thousand mattresses. It created an unbelievable dust storm inside the barracks, and in one stroke everyone lost all his personal possessions.

After all the mattresses had been thrown together, and gotten even dirtier than before and, also, soaking wet, we had to file by one by one and pick up a mattress for ourselves at random. The worst part was not losing our possessions, but drawing a mattress that might be infested with lice, or diptheria, or dysentery, or T.B. Such diseases were all rampant in the camp. Many of us ended up with mattresses more repulsive than the ones that we had been using. I won't attempt to describe what they looked or smelled like. The great mattress switch was only one way that the administration kept us "profitably occupied" in our spare time.

From the beginning, insofar as it was in my power, I concentrated on saving my strength in order to survive as long as possible, for I didn't believe in an early invasion nor in a speedy end to the war. When I considered my situation, things did not look hopeful. I was no longer among the strongest. In a few months, even under conditions more tolerable than those endured by most prisoners, I had weakened significantly. If this continued a few months more or another half year, what would become of me? And although I hoped that, as a clergyman, I would stay in Amersfoort, I was nevertheless uneasy about that matter. My uneasiness appeared justified when Prof. Brandsma, Rev. Hinloopen, and Rev. Kapteyn were all shipped out—to

Scheveningen, it was said. But from there, where to? As we later found out, from Scheveningen they were shipped to Dachau. The future looked dark.

A few prisoners were in Amersfoort who, before they obtained one or another camp function here, had been in Buchenwald. They told us stories that made our skins crawl. Amersfoort was a nursery school by comparison. All prisoners in German camps were treated as the Jews were treated at Amersfoort. And we had seen enough of this to know what it was like. The Jewish Kommando was the kommando to which one was assigned for punishment. One squad pulled a heavy earth roller all day and was constantly beaten and driven with sticks by a half-dozen S.S. They never moved fast enough to suit the S.S. Another squad hauled rocks from one end of camp to the other. Along the path that they had to travel stood S.S. men spaced about twenty yards apart, each armed with a whip or club to beat the prisoners. Elsewhere, the same thing was going on, with the guards using iron pipes. This is what life was like for those in German camps, we were told. It was not a picture that would inspire optimism.

The struggle against the church was gradually being intensified, and the measures being taken against uncooperative preachers were becoming increasingly harsh. We therefore speculated that perhaps all clergymen would eventually be sent to German camps. However, we still clung to one hope and comfort, God's Word.

Pascal once remarked that faith has reasons whereof reason knows nothing. The intellect can reason, draw conclusions, and tremble, while faith meditates on what the intellect does not understand. It does so as described in Hebrews 11, when Abraham by faith was ready to offer up his only son: "He considered that God was able to raise men even from the dead."

The intellect of Abraham could only reason that if he followed God's command to offer up his son, then God's promises could not be fulfilled; for it was through Isaac that

How the Jews were treated.

he was to become a great and mighty nation. Yet Abraham was given the supra-rational and supra-human strength to do what was apparently sub-rational and sub-human; for faith has its own reasons of which reason knows nothing. Faith believes that God is able to raise men even from the dead.

It was this same faith that continually gave us the strength to carry on with hearts unconquered by gloom and despair. After but a few months, however, I could see that I had traveled better than half the distance to the grave. And what would the future bring? Thank God, faith takes other factors into account. The most important, the all-determining factor I had been leaving out, namely, God. I had to rediscover life through that beautiful chapter, II Corinthians 1. Here Paul, in accordance with all reasonable human calculations, draws up his last will and testament. He says that he is living under a death sentence. But to these reasonable calculations faith adds: "But that was to make us rely on God who raises the dead."

Developing this same theme, I preached a sermon on John 21:18-22 in order to comfort both myself and others if we should be shipped off unexpectedly. As God intended, the sermon was given just a few days before we were transported to Germany.

> "Truly, truly, I say to you, when you were young, you girded yourself and walked where you would; but when you are old, you will stretch out your hands, and another will gird you and carry you where you do not wish to go." (This he said to show by what death he was to glorify God.) And after this he said to him, "Follow me." Peter turned and saw following them the disciple whom Jesus loved, who had lain close to his breast at the supper and had said, "Lord, who is it that is going to betray you?" When Peter saw him, he said to Jesus, "Lord, what about this man?" Jesus said to him, "If it is my will that he remain until I come, what is that to you? Follow me!"

Christ here prophesies to Peter that in his latter days he will be shipped off, put in chains, thrown into prison, and that in the end he will be martyred. But Peter will have none of it. It goes contrary to his boldness and aggressiveness, on the one hand, and to his fearfulness, on the other. In the night that he denied his Savior out of fear for himself, he showed his agreement with what Erasmus later wrote to Luther: "I haven't the flesh of a martyr."

Nevertheless, this same Simon Peter, the man with the big mouth and the small heart, became a prisoner and a martyr for Christ's sake. God was able to form out of this man, who had behaved so cowardly, a hero of faith. Peter did not die as a passive victim, but as a martyr, for in his death he glorified God. A miracle! One to give us hope too! In ourselves we really do not possess the flesh and blood of martyrs. Our hearts grow resistant at the thought of dying slowly and miserably of malnutrition and exhaustion. From the human point of view, it seems too tragic. Sometimes the thought of such a death became so oppressive that we wanted to run at the barbed wire like madmen. We wanted to compel God to rain down fire from heaven to destroy the entire satanic tribe of tormenters.

But Christ teaches us to live by a totally different impulse. To glorify God with the greatest sacrifice a man can give—his own life—is a privilege accorded only to a blessed few. And we might be among them. We can understand this viewpoint only if we know that God has blazed the trail for us with the greatest sacrifice of all—the crucifixion of His Son so that we might be forgiven.

But then we must not react the way that Peter did at the crucial moment. He didn't understand the seriousness of the situation and of the words of Christ. His Savior had shown him the only way of accomplishing a God-glorifying martyrdom: follow me! If Peter didn't follow Jesus in full self-surrender, his life would come to nothing. He would only end up denying the Lord once again instead of confessing His name unto death. But Peter is concerned about things that aren't any of his business. His attention is diverted from the seriousness of his own calling by his curiosity about the destiny of someone else: what's going to happen to John?

In this respect, we must not be like Peter. We must not be wrongfully concerned about our neighbor's or brother's life. What business of ours is it if God seems to give one man an easier time in life than another? What business is it of mine if God sets you free tomorrow and ships me off to Germany? We must not compare our thorns to our neighbor's roses. Today we do so out of curiosity, tomorrow out of jealousy, and the day after that out of rebelliousness. If we do so, we will never attain a God-glorifying life and death. Do we ourselves know what is good for us? We know what would be most agreeable, but do we know what is good for us? Only our Heavenly Father knows this. Only Christ knows.

To believe, is to follow Christ. To follow Christ is to refrain from dictating the way to God. But if we follow wherever He goes, then afterward, perhaps only in eternity, we will see that it was good, wholly good. It is good when He gives us much, good when He takes away much. As Luther once put it, "God often deprives us of silver in order to give us gold later." Let us not complain, then, if God deprives us of silver. Let us have the vision of faith to see beyond the momentary setbacks, for His taking away always serves His giving; losing silver enables us to receive gold later on. Only through loss do we profit. Only . . . follow me!

Transport Trials

On Wednesday, at a quarter past twelve, a friend working in the clothing room came to tell me that he had just finished packing bags for sixty-five prisoners who were being transported to Germany. My number was among them, number 230. I had just started my bowl of soup, but my appetite disappeared completely. However, common sense told me to finish eating, a feat that I accomplished.

When we fell in for our 1:30 roll call, the sixty-five numbers were called out. Camp scuttlebutt had it that this would be a "rough transport." The composition of the group wasn't very reassuring either. Forty of the men were Jews with large *R's* stitched on their clothes. The *R* stood for race offender. They were treated even worse than the Jews who were not marked with an *R*. What was their crime? What moral outrage had they committed? These Jews were treated as criminals by the S.S. because they had married non-Jewish women or were engaged to do so. This was the most heinous crime that could be committed against the pure and noble German race.

Among them was a young man who had just married a non-Jewish girl. He had become engaged about ten days before the law banning such marriages had been passed. So he had gone to city hall to ask if it also applied to his marriage. "Of course not," he was told. According to the usual legal norms, his agreement had preceded the new regulation and therefore that law did not apply to him. But the Nazi state wasn't concerned with justice, not even according to its own laws. Intoxicated with power, it did as it pleased. This young man, an exemplary citizen, was convicted by the retroactive impact of the law. He was branded a vile race offender.

As I said, it was a "rough transport." Besides the race offenders there were also twenty committed communists. And, finally, there were five clergymen: De Geus, Idema, Sietsma, Tunderman, and I. There was also one man I haven't mentioned: Mr. Wirtz, a Roman Catholic journalist, who had once given an interesting speech on the Russian revolution, which he had experienced first hand. His presence didn't make things look any better. A week before, he had had a violent confrontation with the camp commandant. The commandant had been beside himself with rage and had shouted that anyone who banged heads with the S.S. had better know that one or the other would end up with a broken head—and he made it clear that it wasn't going to be the commandant. So now Wirtz was with us.

Never had I seen a less promising transport leave the camp. The consensus was that we would all be sent to an extermination camp and be finished off in short order. Subsequent events proved that this was substantially accurate. Of the sixty-five men deported, no more than five survived. As God would have it, they were Mr. Wirtz, Rev. Idema, two of the communists, and I.

Our fellow prisoners were marched off to work in their kommandos. The sixty-five of us left behind had to strip off the uniforms that we had been issued when we entered the camp and to put on our own clothes. For the first time, we really noticed how much weight we had lost in the past three months. Our clothes hung around us in great loose folds.

Nevertheless, it felt good to be wearing decent, relatively clean clothing.

We were informed that we would have to be up at 3:00 A.M. Thursday to leave Amersfoort. That evening, we were free to say our farewells to our friends in the barracks. We all wept, both the men who were leaving and those who were to remain. We had undergone a great deal together. We had preached much and prayed with each other and counselled many others on a one-to-one basis. Now, five pastors were leaving at one time, each of whom had his own flock in the camp.

And I must admit, when we stood there as the social pariahs, as outcasts condemned to death, it took some time of prayer and struggle for me to accept this dreaded tragedy. But then I was lifted above it. The words of Jesus, "Follow me!" spoke to me very intimately. And that evening, the friends from whom I would have to part seemed much sadder than I; and I was thankful that God had enabled me to forget myself and comfort them.

I reminded them of Luther's adage: "God often deprives us of silver in order to be able to give us gold." God was depriving me of my relatively comfortable spot in Amersfoort, but soon He would give me gold, I said. Of what the gold would consist, I didn't know. I told my friends that it could even be that in some way my lot might be improved; I might even be given the gold of freedom.

But possibly God would give me the most beautiful gold of all: that final deliverance from the sufferings of this life. That was all right with me too, I continued. I didn't know what form the gold would take, but I did know that I would receive it soon. "So we are always of good courage," I told them, for "if God is for us, who can be against us?" (II Cor. 5:6; Rom. 8:31).

The next morning we were roused at 3:30. For our trip to Germany (we were not, of course, told to which camp we were going), we received a sizeable loaf of bread, an ounce of butter, an ounce of cheese, and an ounce of meat. That was a feast! Several of the men were so famished that they devoured the whole ration before we had even left camp. Our camp elder warned us against doing just that, however, because he knew what such a transport as the one we faced could entail. It could take days, even weeks, before we reached our destination, and there might be little or no food provided. The majority of us played it smart, therefore, and resolved to be very sparing in the consumption of our food ration.

One of the prisoners had even taken the trouble to cut his bread into neat slices, and he had buttered them and made sandwiches with his precious supply of cheese and meat. But he had not secured them properly in his pack. So at 5 A.M. when we marched off to the Amersfoort station accompanied by twenty disgruntled guards, the entire ration slipped out, the neat slices scattered all over the road. The man made a frantic attempt to save some of them, but one of the guards used his rifle to club him back into line and then ground the sandwiches underfoot. In the train, we all gave up some of our supply so that the man had a ration after all.

We were put into a clean third-class coach and were soon following the route from Amersfoort to Arnhem via Utrecht. It wasn't long before the train was standing at the platform of the Arnhem station. While we were there, I recognized several familiar faces, including some members of my congregation who were waiting for the 8 o'clock train. But although they walked right past our coach and scanned the prisoner transport, they didn't recognize me. My head had been shaved bald, and I had lost a lot of weight. A young man at whose marriage I had officiated only a half year earlier was working on the platform. I motioned to him several times. He made it a practice to look over every prisoner transport to see whether there were Arnhemmers aboard. Then he would signal to them to drop notes or letters out of the train, and after the train left, he would look for them along the tracks, pick them up and deliver them.

Finally he recognized me. He immediately realized that my

wife would wish to be told and went flying off the platform to find a telephone. I was in a state of anxiety lest the train should leave before she could get there. In God's providence, fifteen minutes later I saw her coming, accompanied by our house guests. That I was being transported to Germany came as a great shock to my wife for she had expected me home at any time. The Gestapo officers in The Hague as well as in Arnhem had convinced her that I might be returning soon. At home, my wife had suitcases packed and ready to go so that the family could go on a vacation together in order to give me a chance to recuperate. Now this!

The suffering of the prisoners' wives, I think, was often greater than of the prisoners. The worry and agony, the uncertainty and anxiety over what loved ones might be suffering in the prison camps was psychologically more painful than the suffering, and we may have had to suffer psychologically from the shameful debasement and intolerable injustice that we were made to endure, but those who remained behind, lonely and uninformed, suffered more.

My wife and I both tried to get permission to speak to each other and to say our goodbyes, but she was rudely shoved away with the usual: "Mensch, kommt gar nicht im Frage!" (Not a chance!) The soldier guarding my group would gladly have given his permission, but he dared not because of the pressure that would have come from his fellow-soldiers and his commandant. So my wife and I were forced to say goodbye from a distance. We were keenly aware that this was very likely the last time that we would see each other, so we drank in as much of each other as we could. Now and then, we would fold our hands and lift them up as a reminder that prayer was our source of strength and comfort.

Half an hour later, the train started to pull out. All that time my wife and I had kept our composure, but it had taken a tremendous amount of nervous energy to do so. We kept waving to each other. For us, it was the same as the last goodbye; the next time we expected to see each other was in eternity.

Even our guard was deeply moved by the scene. He tried to hide his emotions by lighting a cigarette, but it fell to the floor, its end bitten off. A guard with human compassion! He offered a cigarette to each of us in the compartment and gave us a drink of coffee from his canteen. He was one of many whose humanity had not been extinguished and who could still see the awful injustices perpetrated against the innocent by the Nazi regime. But was he man enough to say "No" and to refuse to support the annihilation of guiltless victims?

It is hard to put into words the emotions we felt as we crossed the border into the Nazi homeland, so beautiful in its landscape and cultural traditions, but so repulsive in its political and military ideology. At one time, we had all read reports of people who were dying miserably in German concentration camps; now we ourselves faced a similar fate. We discussed our chances of ever again getting back home alive. Some of us were certain that we would never return. Rev. De Geus was in worse physical condition than anyone else. He was suffering badly from edema resulting from starvation. His feet and legs were already horribly swollen with fluid.

The trip went relatively well until we reached Essen, the large industrial city in the Ruhr. After that, the real trials of our transport began. As a group we had just decided that we would eat some of our bread and cheese when the train lurched to a stop. We hadn't figured on stopping in Essen. Our guards were not allowed to say anything about our destination, so we had already considered four possibilities: Oraniënburg, Buchenwald, Dachau, and the worst—Mauthausen, where, it was known, Jews were immediately destroyed. We expected Mauthausen because most of our transport consisted of R-Jews (race offenders). We feared that we had been put with them to be eliminated as quickly as possible.

At Essen we were received by the local prison guards, who rudely pushed and kicked us into patrol wagons. We noticed that the people gathered at the station looked at us more with apprehension and sympathy than with hate and contempt. Their faces revealed their own oppression. They also were enslaved, so it was apparent already, even as early as June of 1942, that, although Germany was still winning on all fronts, the people were by no means happy and secure. They were groggy from the nightly bombings. Especially in this locality, the Ruhr, we noticed factories emblazoned with the sign, "Wir kapitulieren nie!" (We'll never surrender!). It seemed to be part of a campaign to combat the defeatism obvious in the faces of the people.

Half an hour later we passed through the prison gates. We had seen nothing of the city whatsoever, because the trucks had no windows. We quickly scrambled out, dragging our luggage. Before us stood a huge, ugly prison building. Initially, we were all stuffed into a single large cell that held all sixty-five of us, but with little room to move. This led us to speculate that perhaps we were being held here only to wait for a train to carry us to our final destination. But the constant uncertainty gnawed at us and made us increasingly nervous.

Secrecy was one of the most lethal weapons in the psychological warfare waged by the Gestapo. The prisoner could be sure of nothing. He might end up being executed without even a semblance of a trial; or he might be set free. He could be in prison for only a day; or he could be there for the rest of his life. He could count on nothing but the arbitrariness and injustice of the Gestapo system. This was a drain on both the spiritual and the physical strength of the prisoner. He could not resist making calculations and hoping to be released on such-and-such a date. As a result, he kept experiencing terrible disappointments that sap incredible amounts of energy.

If one fell into the hands of the Gestapo, the best thing to do was to expect the worst. So we told each other, "Let's count on being imprisoned until the end of the war." But who could last that long? Without a miracle, nobody could. We were all exhausted and weak, starved and malnourished.

The speculation that we would return to the station in a few hours to continue our trip turned out to be wrong. At 4 o'clock that afternoon, we had to pick up our baggage from the hallway and bring it to the cellar of the prison. Everything had to be turned in—even our precious ration of bread. Despite fierce hunger pangs, we had eaten very little of it. Some of us managed to hide our food in our luggage, hoping that it would be safe there, and that we would be able to recover it in a few days when we were shipped out again. Those few days, however, turned out to be almost four weeks.

After we had signed the customary pledges, we were dispersed to various cells. The bunks were stacked four high. Everywhere the Nazis ruled, there seemed to be an amazing lack of prison space. The prison in Essen, which had a capacity of three thousand, was holding some fifteen-thousand sufferers. As a result, the conditions and care were infamous. A single cell was not very large to begin with, but now from three to five people were jammed into each.

Moreover, there was already a shortage of almost everything. The guard that locked us up apologized for the lack of mattresses and blankets and added the typical excuse, "War is war." We were thankful that it wasn't winter; but even in summer, sleeping on the floor without blankets is hardly pleasant—especially as we were extremely thin and lacked natural padding.

I shared a cell with Rev. Tunderman from Groningen and with a retired street repairman from Rotterdam. The latter was a committed communist and had picked up all the vocabulary. When we got him going, he would carry on like a demagogue about capitalism, capital goods, exploitation, the bourgeoisie, banks, the proletariat, the self-consciousness of the working classes, political agitation, solidarity, and protest demonstrations. The words came rumbling from deep in his throat, even deeper. After a week in the cell, we received one mattress for the three of us. Tunderman and I deferred to the communist because he was the oldest. We got along well together and never had the slightest trouble.

But the days were long. We were wakened at 5:30 to put our smelly slop pail outside the cell. After we had all "washed" in the same small basin of water, we got our breakfast, which consisted of two very thin slices of rye bread covered with a teaspoon of syrup. Five hours later, about 11:30 A.M., we were given a pint of watery soup. That had to last us for seven hours, until 6:30 P.M. when we received two more thin slices of rye bread. We suffered from hunger pangs all day long—a sickening gnawing in the stomach. At night we couldn't sleep because of hunger and pain. Lack of anything to read made it easy to surrender to boredom, gloomy thoughts, and homesickness.

Rev. Tunderman and I decided that preventive measures had to be taken, for these physical discomforts did nothing to prolong our survival. The symptoms of nervous erosion caused by this kind of life were already visible in the first few days, especially because during the first two weeks we were not let out for air even once. When one of us fell into despondency, his weeping threatened to spread to the others. That wasn't good. We agreed, therefore, that we would observe a strict schedule, so that we would always have something to do and would not have time to yield to despair or to talk constantly about food. We proposed to stretch out our breakfast over two hours. That may seem strange, but we made a contest out of it. We had to spend two hours over two thin slices of bread. We did this by cutting our bread into thirty little pieces, each of which had to last four minutes.

This program had several advantages. First, it made the meal seem bigger than it really was. It also guaranteed that we would get the full food value from our meal. Nothing could be wasted; our bodies must have a chance to absorb as much as possible. Furthermore, for two hours we were kept busy alleviating our hunger pangs. And finally, it whiled away two hours of a long day. By the time breakfast was finished, it was 8:30. Then, at a very slow tempo, in order to use as little energy as possible, we would begin to sweep, dust, and mop our cell. This would take until about 10 o'clock. Then one of us would give a talk on some topic for about three quarters of an hour, followed by debate or discussion. Before we expected it, we would hear the cell doors clanging along the hall. Soup was being served!

We decided to make the soup last one hour. Afterwards, at 12:30 P.M., we tried to sleep for a couple of hours.

At 2:30, it was time for the second talk and discussion. Usually, we couldn't stretch this session out any longer than to 5 o'clock. That left us one-and-a-half hours of torment by hunger, but every day, one day at a time, we made it to 6:30 P.M. Then we would again take two hours over our slices of bread so that we could go to bed, or, rather, to the floor, at 8:30. In between, three times a day, we held our devotions and quietly sang our psalms and hymns.

Our communist friend had little appreciation for spiritual matters, however. He was a Marxist of the old school. For him, religion was the opium of the people and all clergymen were deceivers, keeping the people ignorant so as to fill the pockets of the capitalists and lulling the workers to sleep with promises of eternity. It took several weeks of patient talking and kindly friendship before he came to the conclusion that not all clergymen were deliberate deceivers, and that they too had good intentions toward the working class, many even making personal sacrifices for their sake.

It had never before occurred to this man that if these pampered sons of the bourgeoisie had wanted comfortable lives and wished to be parasites on the worker, they would be better off studying medicine or law than theology, for those professions paid ten times better. He was dumbfounded to learn that as a street repairman he had earned more than many pastors, despite the twelve years of study that they had completed beyond him. His applecart was really upset when he came to understand that as clergymen we did not work just one eight-hour day a week but usually seventy and sometimes ninety hours a week.

So we passed our days in Essen prison. But the nights were

different; they were terrifying! About 11 o'clock every night began several hours of chaos as bombs screamed down and anti-aircraft fire roared back. These bombing raids became even more intense later in the war. The worst of it was that when the ominous wailing of the sirens began, everyone in Essen headed for the bomb shelters, including our guards, but we prisoners remained locked in our cells. There we sat, waiting for a bomb to hit the building. In the event of fire, we would all burn because there was no way of getting out of the cells. Every night, after supper, Rev. Tunderman and I read a passage from Scripture for encouragement, and we prayed for protection and for peace in our souls. Shortly thereafter, the deafening wail of the sirens usually began. The shrill sound of warning came from directly overhead, from the roof of the prison, where an anti-aircraft gun added to the din. The three of us climbed up on the table in our cell to look out of the window. From our vantage point on the fourth floor, we could look out over all of Essen. Every night provided a phantasmagoria of light and sound.

The storm of destruction moved inexorably toward us while we watched and listened. First, it was a rumbling like thunder far in the distance, accompanied by the continuous flashing of anti-aircraft fire and bombs. It came shuddering toward us across the entire expanse of the horizon. A few miles away, the bombs splattered down and exploded, while numerous anchored balloons spooked to and fro across the sky, obstructing the passage of the bombers. There was an almost impenetrable curtain of flak. Here and there, a burning airplane came blazing out of the sky. The scream of German fighters was deafening as they dove at their heavier prey, which spat back torrents of machine-gun fire. But almost drowning out everything else was the throbbing thunder that beat down on the earth and the sharp rattle and twang that answered back.

It was an extremely frightening sight also, for many times we thought, "Now surely we're going to be hit!" All in all, it was a terrible but at the same time fascinating spectacle. The silence following the crackling inferno of fire and noise was just as fearsome. But God took us through each night unscathed.

After about fourteen days, we were allowed our first fresh air. When we entered the hallway, we stared in shock at one another's pale, drawn features. In the exercise yard, we had to march along the high walls in single file at one-yard intervals. A few guards stood in the middle of the yard, watching closely that no one talked or signaled to his neighbor. The whole picture with us trudging in circles like circus animals, suddenly struck me as funny. What a crazy world! If the purpose of this madhouse had not been so gruesome, I would have been inclined to break out into laughter. The fresh air did us good. But we were all tired out, completely exhausted just from that brief march around the yard.

About four weeks after our arrival, we were mustered out to collect our baggage from the cellar. At 3:30 the next morning, we would once again be put on transport. New surprises awaited us! Even if it is far from pleasant, one usually prefers the known to the unknown. What horrors would the future bring? The concentration camps of Oraniënburg, Buchenwald, Dachau, and Mauthausen were getting closer; but we were anxious to see what, if anything, was left of the rations that had been stored away in our luggage for four weeks. We were so hungry that we were willing to eat anything—except spoiled meat, of course. To anyone in our condition, food poisoning would be fatal.

Once our baggage was in our cells, we frantically tore it open to check our rations. The meat was, as we feared, badly spoiled; the cheese was covered with a thick layer of mold, and so was the bread. Nevertheless, we greedily consumed everything except the meat. Finally, we had had a meal that filled our stomachs a little. But it was a miracle of God's mercy that none of us got sick.

Someone who has never suffered from hunger month after month cannot know what it is like. One has to fight constantly not to descend to an animal level, in which all that one can

THE PRISON YARD IN ESSEN.

think of is eating! One lives from one meal to the next, especially when one is locked in a cell where the only stimulation is the inadequate bit of food pushed at you through a serving hatch.

In a book of poems written by prisoners of war, I found the following sonnet that conveys the thoughts of a hungry prisoner:

As feeding time draws near again;
we hover round the door with bulging eyes;
deranged by hunger, abandoning the race of men,
we covet others' bread with beast-like cries.

We measure out our freedom, pacing in a pen.
The day drones on like madly buzzing flies.
In here, we feed on our own excrement—
the human spirit, the heartbeat of creation dies.

Others stand, like us, at doors not far away,
their faces growing hollower day by day;
their minds, like ours, are food-obsessed.

It's Sunday. Some fill the day with psalms.
The lust for corn-husks in my belly calms;
I hug my knees against my chest, and rest.

What a blessing when, under such circumstances, we are still able to sing psalms. Then man is still aware that he is a spiritual creature, that he is the crown of God's creation. But at such a time we also feel the full weight of the war of the flesh against the spirit.

By 3:30 the next morning, we were already standing at the prison gate. We were hurried into the patrol wagons and driven to the station. A train stood waiting. Coupled to it was a prison car, an almost windowless car with a narrow hall down the center and on either side little cells hardly large enough for one man. High in each cell was a tiny window covered with wire, but the glass was frosted so that the prisoners couldn't see out.

There were about three or four times as many prisoners as cells, but that was of no concern to the Germans. Three or four prisoners, plus their baggage, were crammed into each cell. Once two of us had entered, there was no more room, and the door could hardly close. But, nevertheless, one or two more persons were wedged into each cell. We were kicked and pounded, and the door was shouldered until we were all in. Then the door was locked.

We traveled this way from 4:30 in the morning until 9:30 at night—for 17 hours. A few cell doors were opened during the trip on a stop at Frankfurt am Main. A few giggling waitresses from the station peered in; the soldiers treated them to a little sight-seeing tour. The S.S. guards described us as "die Abscheu der Menschheit" (the abomination of mankind). It was deeply humiliating treatment; but, we reasoned, we were paying them too much respect if we considered them capable of humiliating us. "He who laughs last, laughs best," we told each other in self-defense.

At 9:30 we arrived in Würzburg—beautiful Würzburg where I had once sat on the station terrace with my wife and friends during a vacation trip. Our muscles were now in such bad shape that we couldn't walk or stand. But a prisoner of the Nazis never says, "I can't." All that counts is, "You must!" And if you don't go fast enough, a few blows will speed you up. We were bivouacked in a new prison, in a building that hardly even looked like a prison. It looked more like a police station or an administrative building.

The director didn't expect us. The Germans liked to brag that their organization was flawlessly efficient, but they did blunder every so often. Therefore, we were given nothing to eat after our excruciating trip, nor did we get much of a chance to rest. All sixty-five of us were put in a single room for the night. A few could lie on the floor, but the rest of us had to stand or sit along the walls and try to sleep that way as best we could.

It was a miserable night. The Jews were extremely irritable and quarreled over the slightest thing. As clergymen, we

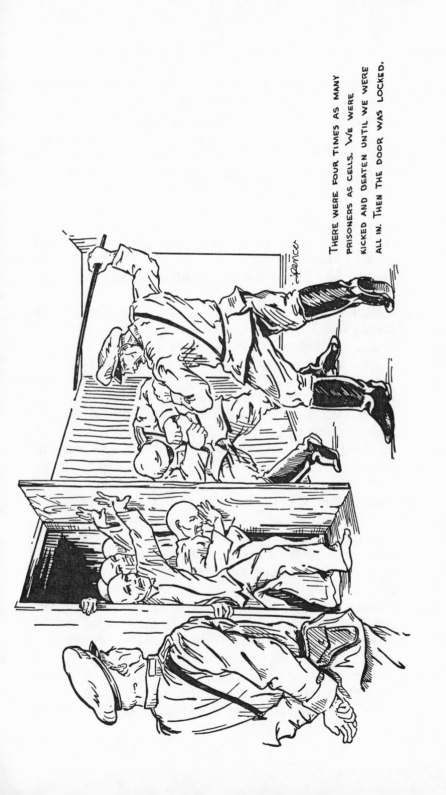

THERE WERE FOUR TIMES AS MANY PRISONERS AS CELLS. WE WERE KICKED AND BEATEN UNTIL WE WERE ALL IN. THEN THE DOOR WAS LOCKED.

decided to assume leadership and try to calm our fellow prisoners. We took turns addressing them on the basis of some text from Scripture. We pointed to the seriousness of the situation, that we might not have long to live; but we emphasized that Jesus Christ offers a place of rest. They all listened quietly, evidently moved by our words. Everyone had a deep need for leadership and comfort that night.

Early the next morning, we were given ten small bowls of water and ten towels, or at least what were supposed to function as towels. Each bowl of water had to be used by at least six men. Most of us preferred to remain unwashed and keep our own filth rather than pick up someone else's disease and filth in addition. Finally, we all had a piece of bread and something that looked like coffee. The Jews were soon ordered out to travel to another destination. As we found out later, none of them survived—not one.

The communists were also called out that morning. They were sent to Grosz-Rosen, an extremely bad camp, where most of them died. Later, in Dachau, I was able to speak to one of these men, a once powerfully-built fellow, who had been sent from Grosz-Rosen to Dachau as an invalid. He told me how the Nazis had disposed of the others. This was in the spring of 1943. I concluded that by then, of the sixty-five men who had been part of the rough transport shipped to Germany in June of 1942, only about a half dozen were still alive. At the end of the war, I could find only three survivors.

We five clergymen were the only ones who stayed behind that morning. We quickly initiated a conversation with a guard who had a sympathetic face. Happily, we had picked the right one, for although he was nervous and fearful, he talked with us, pausing frequently to listen for someone approaching. He told us that we were in a county jail and that he was a Roman Catholic. We then told him who we were, and for what "crimes" we were being shipped to a German concentration camp. The man was astonished! He thought that the Dutch had welcomed the German occupation enthusiastically and gratefully. Even this soldier, who was not a party man and who knew that much of Goebbel's propaganda was false, had believed the lies about the occupation of Holland.

Spiritually we were in excellent shape. We preached to each other every day and sang frequently. It was a beautiful, unforgettable time. After a few days, however, our privileged existence came to an end. A few jaundiced guards had discovered the director's favors to us and, snarling profanities came barging into our cell to confiscate our reading material and put us to work. We were brought piles of caps from soldiers who had been wounded or killed and were told to remove the insignia from the old caps so that they could be put on new ones. The old caps went to the prisoners in the concentration camps. We saw nothing more of the director or of the considerate guard. Our friendship was too dangerous to them. They might be betrayed by party men on the staff, and they might end up in a concentration camp themselves.

After two weeks, the chains were put on again and, fastened in pairs, we were taken to the station along with other prisoners. Once again we were put in a prison car, but this time only two in each cell. That was much better. And the trip was not as long.

We thought that we would be shipped straight through to Dachau, but, instead, we were sent to a huge prison in the famous city of Neurenburg. For two days we endured utter degradation. The prison was a caldron of Europe's sufferings, a melting pot of agony. A huge gymnasium in the prison held thousands of people from all parts of Europe and beyond: Frenchmen, Czechs, Dutchmen, Poles, Germans, Norwegians, Russians, Luxemburgers, Greeks, Belgians, Jews, Italians, even Blacks and Chinese. What country was *not* represented? It was an immense, writhing clot of humanity.

Along the sides of the gym were straw-filled bags on which sprawled hundreds of men, packed so closely that they almost lay on top of one another. Some had found a spot on the

EVERY HUMAN BEING THERE WAS A
PICTURE OF MISERY.

floor for themselves, but not without a battle. Most were forced to stand—and to stand and stand—until they collapsed. Here and there, in the midst of the seething mass, men lay dying. Every day, scurvy, dysentery, and typhoid claimed their corrupted victims. The creatures that thrived in that room were the lice.

The water fountain over in one corner was mobbed day and night as men fought to get a sip of water. Some ten slop pails spread around the room served as latrines, but they were overflowing and as filthy on the outside as on the inside. A nauseating stench permeated everything. It was as if a scene from the bowels of Dante's *Inferno* had come to life.

I decided to assume the detached viewpoint of an observer, as though I had been sent here to cover a story by a newspaper. I managed to climb up on an exercise horse to get an overview of this wretched mass of humanity. I told myself, "The time for outrage and righteous anger is later. You are too weak now. If you give in to your outrage at all this inhumanity, injustice, and degradation, you will be overcome by it, and you will die in no time. You will neither survive, nor will you be able to expose this horror or make an appeal for justice."

Every human being there was in unutterable misery! Each one had suffered heinous abuse before he even arrived. Racked by fear, hounded, arrested, tortured during interrogation, constantly manhandled, lashed by uncertainties, consumed by homesickness, hunger and thirst, pain and exhaustion, and then flung into that boiling, putrid pot. And behind him, each man had left an ocean of grief and confusion to his family and friends. Each prisoner had left behind a wife or fiancée, parents or children, friends and possessions. The thousands of bonds that relate each one of us to his daily life and work had been savagely ruptured for each of us in that room.

I saw everything with double vision, before and after. I saw a sunny house and garden, with a happy, healthy couple quietly drinking tea together after a day's work, while children ran in and out. Then I saw the same man lying wasted on the floor like a pile of filth, wrestling hopelessly with death. I saw priests and pastors serving their churches and being gladly received by their congregations; then I saw them being kicked about like mangy dogs. I also saw strong laborers, office workers, industrialists, members of parliament—then and now.

I saw myself as a boy playing near my mother in the kitchen, and I thanked God that she had been spared these evil times and that she was with Him in heaven. I saw myself in school as a carefree high-school and college student, completely unaware that I would one day be hurled with thousands of others into this hellhole. And I saw myself in my first congregation among farmers and laborers—who were even now perhaps praying for their former pastor. And I saw my second church where my work had been so clearly blessed.

Then I saw the beautiful city of Arnhem, where I should have been serving right now. I saw the congregation, the consistory, the children and the young people, my colleagues. And I saw my home, and my little girl and my wife, sad and worried about my fragile health, powerless to do anything. Was I dreaming or was I awake? Which was the real world? Now or then; here or there? No, I told myself, *this* was reality! I was part of this anguish, and I couldn't escape it. Horrible!

But no, I had resolved to be outraged at nothing. Otherwise, I reminded myself, I didn't have a chance of survival. I could and would endure it! And soon in Dachau, I determined, I would accept even more. When God had led me through this and out of it, then there would be time for outrage. But not now! Now, by His grace, I would not let the filth and evil infect me. Inwardly, I would stay out of reach. They might take my body and encrust it with the corruption of their injustice, but they would never touch my soul, for my soul was in the hands of God. Adjust, and keep an inner distance. Experience it, but let it pass by. Be in the middle of it, but still rise above it. That is the strength that Christ gave me, for he who suffers in Him suffers with a difference. "In all this we are more than conquerors."

Suddenly, a few days after I had thus resolved my turmoil, the announcement came: "Transport Dachau! Silence!" Names were called out, and once again we heard: De Geus, Overduin, Sietsma, Idema, Tunderman, and many more. Once again we gathered our belongings and stood at attention. Once again we were chained together and herded into patrol wagons. The train was waiting for us at the station. A few hours later we arrived in Dachau.

I hardly have to point out that we suffered severely from the transport. Our physical strength was nearly gone. And now we were entering the unknown but not-unheard-of world of Dachau.

The Secrets of Dachau

A little prayer was then current in Germany which went thus:

"Lieber Jesu, mach' mir fromm,
Dass ich nicht nach Dachau komm."
(Dear Jesus, make me good now
so I don't end up in Dachau.)

Dachau was the epitome of all the depravity and diabolism that could overcome a person. The average German did not know exactly what went on in this concentration camp, but he did know that in it everything inhuman was practiced and praised.

Dachau was the oldest—or one of the oldest—of the concentration camps. It seems to have been founded in 1933, when Hitler seized power. During the span of its existence, hundreds of thousands of innocent people were tortured to death within its confines.

If the stones of its streets, the walls and floorboards of its barracks could speak, they would scream for revenge because of the blood that was shed there. If the straw mattresses could tell the agony of all the men who died on them, what a raucous chorus that would be! And if the crematorium could speak, it would hiss, "I've lost count, I've burnt so many—not only the dead, but also the living!" Many who collapsed from exhaustion or from beatings were tossed among the dead and carted off to the crematorium on dump trucks.

Dachau was located 17 kilometers north of Munich on the Bavarian plateau. It comprised the city of Dachau and the village of Dachau, which together had fewer than 20,000 inhabitants. The people were predominantly Roman Catholic, as they were elsewhere in Bavaria. The camp was a half-hour's walk from the city limits and was surrounded by a huge complex of S.S. barracks and other S.S. buildings. These usually housed about 20,000 troops, consisting of the guards, the administrative personnel, the officers, the new recruits, and the hospital staff. It was impossible for civilians to see the camp, even from a distance.

The huge S.S. grounds, including many gates and check points, lay before the high barbed-wire fence that marked the entrance to the concentration camp itself. This fence was charged with an electrical current so powerful that anyone who attempted to escape would be immediately burnt to a cinder. The entrance was a big brick structure that contained several rooms for offices and for guards to sleep in. Set into the brick entrance was a heavy, wrought-iron gate adorned with the words: "Arbeit macht frei!" (labor brings freedom)—one of the delusions that the Nazis tried to propagate among the prisoners. We all labored all right—until we dropped dead! But labor brought freedom to no one. "Labor brings freedom, all right—through the chimney," said the camp wits, meaning the smokestack of the crematorium. Only death brought freedom in Dachau.

Once through the gate, one saw a huge parade square. It was so large that it could easily accommodate a hundred thousand men. On the right side stood a large brick building with two wings. In the middle was a tremendous kitchen with all the latest equipment. Next to it were the baths, in which

Only death brought freedom at Dachau.

600 men could shower at the same time. On the other side of the kitchen was the potato-peeling room, where vegetables were also prepared for cooking. Next to it, was a very modern laundry. The right wing held the administrative department, which took care of the personal possessions and clothing of new arrivals. Prison clothing and shoes were stored in the left wing. The attic was a huge closet containing all the civilian clothing of the prisoners, whereas the basement housed the camp tailors, shoemakers, and stocking-darners.

When you turned your back to this huge, somber, brackish-green building, you looked across the vast parade ground down the long, broad main street of the camp. It was lined on both sides by tall black poplars, like those found in many cemeteries. At right angles to the main street stood thirty barracks, or blocks, for the prisoners, fifteen on each side, the even numbers on the left, and the odd on the right.

Block number 2 was a display room containing all kinds of interesting statistics and documents about the camp. This block was not for the prisoners but for visiting dignitaries. However, we used to peek through the windows occasionally. Among the exhibits were skulls of "criminal types," for example, gypsies and Jews. The second floor of this block was a canteen where formerly one could get some rather worthwhile things; but in 1942 and after, about all that it sold was food products made almost entirely of water.

Block 4 housed the Labor Pool, the office that provided work for each of the fifteen-to twenty-thousand prisoners in the camp in 1942-1943, assigning each man to a work kommando.

The "Prominents," the powerful and influential among the prisoners, lived together in Block 6. They were mostly communists and old-timers; a small number of them had been there since 1933. They belonged to the few dozen who had survived the first terrible year—a few dozen out of tens of thousands. As a reward they were given positions in the camp, such as Capo (foreman of a work kommando), Stubenälteste (room elder), Blockälteste (block elder),

Schreiber (bookkeeper for a block or kommando), Sanitäter (orderly in one of the hospital blocks).

These people had a livelihood. They received extra bread, meat, and butter rations; they didn't have to work hard; and through their close ties to the kitchen help, they had the opportunity to "organize" even more food. In contrast to the other prisoners, they usually looked pretty good and were usually hardened and strengthened by their Spartan existence. They wielded a great deal of power in the camp, and they could even determine the life or death of their fellow prisoners. If they were somewhat compassionate, they could arrange lighter work for an exhausted prisoner so that he would not be literally worked to death.

Most of the Prominents were not compassionate, however, and they demanded the impossible. Through their bullying and vituperation, thousands of victims were hurried along to an early grave. Years of misery had so warped them and hardened them to the atrocities in the camp that they no longer cared about another's life. It was, for them, just one man more or less— it made little difference in the functioning of the camp. For every man lost today, they could collect ten replacements tomorrow at the slave market of the Labor Pool. The work kommandos were always filled. The dead were replaced every day.

Among the room and block elders there were some real beasts. This was true also of the orderlies; some would even eat the rations of the sick. These men, if any are still alive, must have a great many deaths on their consciences. But the more they adopted the methods of the S.S., the better was their standing with the camp leaders, and the easier it was for them at the time. These jobs were not for men with compassion and a sense of justice.

Yet, we thanked God, there were exceptions. In particular I recall Julius who worked in the Labor Pool. He never tired of trying to accommodate people's weaknesses when he assigned jobs. It took almost six months before I had a chance to talk to him. Similarly, Willy Bader, the room elder of the Admission Block played a big role in keeping me alive. He was tough, but he had a strict sense of justice. He also possessed an extensive knowledge of people, and it did not take him long after the arrival of a new transport to discover what kind of men he was dealing with.

Everyone trembled when he exploded in his almost unintelligible German dialect. But my colleague Idema and I soon established a good relationship with him, and it wasn't long before we were discussing all kinds of problems together. Bader had been a communist member of the city council in Stuttgart; he had been imprisoned since 1933. Possessed of a sharp intellect, he had read much, if somewhat one-sidedly, and he wasn't a bad poet. He was a pantheist, which for him meant virtually the same thing as being atheist; he defended the values and truths of Christianity, but without Christ.

In Blocks 8 through 30 (the rest of the even-numbered Blocks) lived Germans, Czechs, and Yugoslavs, coded by black badges, green badges, and red badges, respectively.

Each prisoner was issued a prison uniform, a so-called zebra suit, which resembled striped pajamas. On the left side, the jacket and pants were marked with one's prison number and a small triangle of colored cloth—red, pink, black, yellow, green, blue, or purple. Each color had a special significance. Red signified a political prisoner; pink, a homosexual; black, an asocial or shirker; yellow, a Jew; green, career criminal; blue, volunteer for the Allies; purple, Jehovah's Witness. There were also the preventive prisoners, prisoners who had committed no crime, but who, it was assumed, would commit a crime under certain conditions. These were put in preventive detention.

The honorary prisoners were those who had done distinguished service for the Third Reich either before or during their imprisonment. They wore purple armbands, were allowed to let their hair grow, got enough to eat, had an easy job or no job at all, and lived apart from the rest of us in separate rooms. Rev. Niemöller and Shuschnigg were both honorary prisoners. They got food from the S.S. kitchen, didn't have to work, sat apart from the rest of the prisoners and had no contact with them. They were also permitted to read and study. Staying alive was no problem for them.

Prisoners with black and white circles stitched on their uniforms were the unhappy ones who had been assigned to a penal kommando for different periods of time. Most of them never got out of their kommandos alive. A red circle meant that the prisoner had been accused, rightly or not, of attempting to escape. Block elders, room elders, foremen, and camp elders could also be distinguished by their arm bands, and by their exceptionally good health.

Block 26 housed all the German clergymen. It consisted of three sitting rooms, three bedrooms, and a chapel, which only they were permitted to use. (The source of this privilege I will explain later.) Polish clergymen stayed in Blocks 28 and 30; between 1940 and 1943, they were the worst barracks in the entire camp.

Across the main street of the camp were the odd-numbered Blocks: 1 to 29. Of these, Blocks 1 to 13 were taken by the infirmary, which did not exist until 1943. At times, only one or two blocks were set aside for the sick. There was a first-aid room, an X-ray unit, an operating room, and a dentist's office. There were also rooms for those with hunger edema, phlegmon (lesions), diphtheria, typhoid, paratyphoid, scurvy, venereal disease, scarlet fever, T.B., skin diseases, dysentery, and other communicable illnesses.

The accommodations for the patients were extremely poor. Here, too, everyone was stacked on bunks three high—it was just another warehouse for human beings! Every straw mattress had already served as a deathbed for hundreds of people who had died of any number of ailments, many of them leaving their contagions behind. As soon as a patient died, he was carried away in his sheet to the autopsy room for tests, and his corpse was burnt the following day. Immediately, another patient was put on his mattress. It was better not to think about such things, though.

An S.S. doctor dropped in for an hour or so every day, but

he gave only minimum supervision to the infirmary, and handled almost no patients himself. The sick were really doctored by the Sanitäters, the orderlies, who were there more for the sake of the position than out of consideration for the sick. They made all the diagnoses and provided treatments, but none were doctors. Before they came to the camp, they had been shoemakers, laborers, miners—anything but trained doctors.

So, of course, serious mistakes were made in the infirmary. We were warned: Never go to the infirmary! It means certain death. The chances of getting out of the infirmary alive were miniscule. One reason, to be sure, was that no one was admitted until he was near death. But there were other reasons. For example, since the sick were unproductive, many were simply given a shot to hasten death. And, also, the infirmary exposed a person to a whole gamut of contagious diseases.

Associated with the infirmary was the "research lab," where prisoners were vivisected, that is, subjected to experimental operations. The lab was directed by a professor from Berlin, a man thoroughly indoctrinated by Nazism. He preferred human beings to rats, mice, or rabbits for his scientific experiments. He used not only sick prisoners, but also healthy ones. Our hearts pounded with dread every time we heard the shout, "Antreten!" (fall in). We stood in rows, like defenseless sheep for the slaughter. A few men in white coats appeared, and we knew the kind of gruesome fate that threatened us. Once again, subjects were being selected to serve as living, human guinea pigs for the professor. Usually fifty to one hundred men were taken at one time. "Is it my turn to go?" each prisoner wondered.

To see the victims marched off to the infirmary was fearful! Under what kind of pain and torture would they die? And if they did live, would they be maimed for life?

Research was being done on malaria when I arrived at the camp. A number of containers with infected mosquitoes were placed on the prisoner's body to infect him. When he was thoroughly in the grip of a malarial fever, the professor came along with all his serums. These potent concoctions were injected into the prisoner's blood stream. Then the professor would wait to see what the reaction would be, meticulously recording all his observations. In this manner, he served the cause of science. During my five-week stay in the infirmary, I saw malaria patients who were unrecognizable because of the sores that covered them from head to foot. They moaned night and day. Many of them died because of the experiments performed on them.

Another experiment involved the artificial creation of phlegmon. This is a condition in which deep sores develop as a result of hunger edema. A person suffering from starvation for a long time first becomes very skinny. He literally becomes skin and bones—a living skeleton! Then he begins to gain weight again. But it is a dangerous weight gain, for it results from the collection of fluids in the tissues under the skin. If this fluid stays there long enough, it turns into pus. The skin disintegrates, and a lesion opens in the skin from the inside out.

Anyone who had swollen legs and hands, a puffy face and blisters under his eyes was in this stage of starvation. He was nearing death. The phlegmon stage would certainly follow soon. It was really a kind of localized death and disintegration resulting from a lack of vitamins and other necessary nutrients. I myself passed through all these stages in Dachau. It was a time of deep anguish, for I knew exactly how close to death I was. People at various stages of starvation were all around me; hence, I could judge exactly how far along toward death I was.

First, came the drastic weight loss and the appearance of being just skin and bones. Next, came the loss of sensation in the feet and legs, and, especially, continuously cold feet, and after that a prickling in the feet, a symptom of fluid. This was followed by swollen legs, and, finally, by phlegmon. These lesions caused tremendous pain. There was no chance that they would heal in camp either, because phlegmon could be cured only by a fortified diet and a high intake of vitamins. In

1942, there was no chance of that. When we began receiving Red Cross packages in 1943, however, quite a few prisoners recovered from phlegmon, but very slowly.

Meanwhile, in the lab the magnificent discovery had been made that phlegmon could be induced artificially in prisoners who were not yet in the last stages of starvation. These artificially created ulcers made it impossible for the subjects to sit, stand, or lie down without excruciating pain. This in itself was bad enough, but then came the "treatments." All kinds of antidotes were tried—mostly numerous injections, which usually only aggravated the prisoner's condition. These mad, inhuman experiments destroyed even more lives than the malaria induction.

Experiments were also performed to measure sexual response to hot and cold water. I won't describe these, however, because I don't know how to do so and preserve decency.

To test the effects of decreasing air pressure on human beings, prisoners were put in a large bell jar. Gradually more and more air was pumped from the jar, so that finally the prisoners' blood vessels would burst.

An example of experimentation on a different level took place in a mental ward in the camp. Nervous exhaustion and mental breakdowns were quite common in Dachau. Such cases, most of which could easily have been cured with proper treatment, were herded together into one big room—the mental ward. When between fifty and one hundred mental patients had been collected, they would be turned outside one day, disoriented, numbed, and confused, and be herded to the showers. After they had had a shower and a bowl of cabbage soup, they were driven either to the gas chamber or to the strangulation chamber. In the latter, a necklace was put around the patient's neck and activated electronically, tightening until the victim strangled to death.

All this was consistent with what we were told by the S.S. officer who "welcomed" us: "Remember, a prisoner is worth less than these paving stones under my feet; I can at least walk on them. But you—you're all a bunch of useless parasites!"

We soon discovered what happened to those persons designated psychopaths, mental patients, and those with nervous disorders, mental deficiencies, and physical deformities in the Third Reich. The earlier "institutions of mercy" were being phased out. The S.S. would have nothing to do with the Christian idea of mercy. They despised it! An S.S. man was drilled to be hard, ever harder, and always hard.

As in Amersfoort, there were times when everyone was ordered to be present at roll call, even those who were normally excused. Perhaps the count had not tallied—no one ever knew the reasons. But even the critically ill, those with pneumonia and high fevers—all were ordered out into the cold winter air, supported by orderlies. Some died immediately from the shock.

One night, several half-drunk S.S. men visited one of the infirmary blocks occupied by seriously ill patients. Outside, lay a thick layer of snow. The patients wore nothing but flimsy hospital gowns. The S.S. men ordered them to muster outside; and then these severely ill men were made to roll around in the snow and do all kinds of exercises. I don't remember the number exactly, but I believe that less than half of them made it through the night.

As a prisoner, one awoke every morning not knowing what new horrors lay ahead. Any moment one might become a victim of a sadistic whim of the S.S. To imagine these vicious humiliations is impossible if you have not experienced them. You are no longer master of your own body; you are a plaything of someone else's perversity, of a demonic spirit in human form. He can do with you whatever enters his demented brain. Reliable witnesses told me of things that happened before 1942, before my arrival in Dachau, which are too barbaric to put into words. I knew a number of prisoners, charged with sex offences, who had been castrated. The S.S. had more ways of maiming human beings than anyone would ever want to imagine.

Fellow prisoners once told me about a hospital train that arrived in Dachau carrying sick prisoners from Buchenwald, supposedly for recuperation. It was winter, and on the Dachau plateau, the temperature was about 30 degrees below zero (-22°F). Moreover, heavy snowfalls were quite frequent. About four hundred sick wretches were detrained in the vacation spot of Dachau. They were all herded into an unfinished garage; the walls were up, but the roof had not yet been put on. There they spent several nights and days. They climbed on top of one another for warmth, but gradually all of them froze to death. They were left to freeze and were buried under a blanket of snow. Thus they became one solid mass of frozen flesh. Later, prisoners were sent in with picks to break the bodies apart and cart them off to the crematorium. The dead prisoners' families all received notices: "Died of pneumonia" or "Died of dysentery."

One day I saw a prisoner who was almost dead, crawling to the infirmary because he couldn't walk. He was turned away by the orderlies, even refused a mattress to die on. When he cried out in terrible misery, he was kicked away from the building. He died the next day at roll call.

The roll call numbers always had to tally. You were either dead or alive. There was no in-between condition recognized. Even the dead who had not yet been written off had to appear at roll call.

At 4 o'clock every afternoon, the bookkeeper of every block had to report the number of prisoners present to the Labor Pool. One day about report time, one of the prisoners was found prostrate and choking on the ground by the toilets. He was dying. But would he be alive for the 7 P.M. roll call or not? He belonged neither to the dead nor to the living. Nor did he belong to the sick, for he was not registered at the infirmary.

This situation was intolerable in the concentration camp. Above all, the numbers had to tally! Bookkeeping came before people; numbers before lives. So the block elder took a pail of water and poured it into the dying man's open mouth. He drowned. Now he belonged to the dead. The bookkeeping problem had been solved and the report would agree with the roll call.

But I was describing the layout of the camp. After Blocks 1 to 13 came Block 15, the Admission Block for newly arrived prisoners. Here they were broken in and initiated. This initiation process I will describe in more detail in the next chapter.

The next odd-numbered blocks housed Russians and, later on, Italians. They had it very rough. Last of all came the Invalid Blocks. The prisoners did everything they they could to stay out of the infirmary because the risk of death was very great; but neither did they want to end up in the Invalid Block, at least not prior to 1943. Crammed into this block were the moving corpses, those who had given up, those who simply, physically, could not go on, and those who had been dragged here against their will because they were no longer productive.

They got the same amount of food as the other prisoners, and smaller demands were made on their remaining energy. So, in a certain sense, they had an advantage. One might think that they could last longer under such conditions. All other things being equal, this would perhaps be true. But accommodations in this block were even more miserable than those in the regular blocks. They were even more crowded, if that were possible. A single straw mattress had to be shared by two or three invalids and, sometimes, even by four or five. All the residents were sick and thoroughly exhausted, so they had no resistance. All kinds of diseases and infections, therefore, raged unchecked. Everyone contaminated everyone else. Prisoners died wholesale.

I have seen quite a few photos of Belsen, Buchenwald, and Dachau, taken after the war to give people some idea of the inhuman conditions in the camps. But I said to myself, what I saw was much worse, much more searing. When, for example, the residents of the Invalid Block stumbled by on their way to the showers in their foul underwear and tattered

THOSE ABOUT TO DIE, GREET YOU.

rags, hanging onto one another for support, it was a parade of several hundred skeletons covered with scurvy and rashes, pimples and boils, lesions and sores. We said to ourselves, "Moriture te salutant!" (Those about to die, greet you!) It was horrifying to see that these skeletons were still alive, that these specters could still move. "Were we in the realm of the dead?" we asked ourselves.

But why talk about invalids, for when we, the working prisoners, went to the showers as a block of six or seven hundred men at a time, did we look that much better? I myself weighed no more than 80 pounds, including the weight of the water collected in my legs. My normal weight was 170. We must have made a grotesque picture: all those deformed bodies, puffed-up heads, arms like sticks, jutting pelvises and ribs, bellies swollen with water, thighs you could encircle with one hand, huge knee joints and great ballooning lower legs that had lost all shape, and skins mottled with discoloring, disfiguring eruptions.

Almost everyone was covered with bleeding and suppurating sores, pustules, boils, and lesions; so to share two hundred showers among six hundred men was a nauseating experience. You walked around in one another's blood and filth. Once when I expressed my revulsion, a barber who had been in the Grosz-Rosen camp said, "Man, this is ideal compared to Grosz-Rosen! There you were flung or shoved into one huge bathtub with between twenty and thirty other men, and soon you were splashing around in water red with blood and stinking with pus. That was called taking a bath!"

To come back to the invalids for a moment: the worst to befall anyone was to be counted out of the work force and to be classified as a good-for-nothing, a parasite. That was impermissible in the great German Reich. You had a right to food and life, only if you did something for the state. Once you were squeezed out like an orange rind, you were thrown out with the other waste. You were designated *garbage*! That was the cold-blooded economics of National Socialism— much more callous than the ruthless application of capital-

BLOCK 28 TAKES A BATH.

ism, for although the latter system wants nothing to do with social equality, at least it is willing to speak of philanthropy and to encourage humanitarian relief projects.

The Nazi system was built on lies, on a semblance of righteousness. No one had the courage to come right out and tell the truth, namely, that these invalids were to be exterminated! No, these poor wretches were repeatedly loaded on transports with unknown destinations. Where to? For what purpose? Were they being shipped to the gas chambers? Of course not! we were told. They were simply being transferred to a sanitorium to speed their recovery. Or they were being sent to another camp with better accommodations, better food, better medical facilities for rest and recuperation.

But it was all a demonic deception. They were hauled from one camp to another, all right: from Dachau to Buchenwald, from Buchenwald to Oraniënburg, from Grosz-Rosen and Neuengamme to Dachau, back and forth, again and again. Hundreds died along the way. They were packed into sealed boxcars so tightly that it was impossible to lie down and sleep. There they stayed, often for a whole week, and sometimes longer, sometimes in the bitter cold of winter, and sometimes in the torrid heat of summer.

Conditions in the boxcars were worse than bestial. Even before the invalids got to the station from which they were to be transported, several had already died from the baths and the long waits. But the books had to balance. If the register said 768 invalids to Dachau, even if twenty had already died before departure, 768 men were shipped to Dachau—including the twenty bodies. And every hour of the journey more dead bodies were added to the transport.

One of my friends in the camp, who had experienced one such trip coming from Buchenwald to Dachau, told me that for eight days and nights he had sat on a body. He had had no choice; it was the only place he could sit. And how often the surviving invalids tried to alleviate their hunger by gnawing the bones of their just-deceased comrades. A multitude of vagabonds, of outcasts, of good-for-nothings was created and then allowed to die bit by bit. The Invalid Blocks were therefore kept in strict isolation. No other prisoners were allowed to visit or even to look into these blocks.

This changed in 1943. Then I was allowed to visit the Invalid Blocks every day to bring food from our packages. Many victims were able to recover. By then, invalids were no longer shipped here and there and everywhere. The Nazis saw that they might lose the war, and they were getting worried about their own skins. Hundreds of invalids recovered to such an extent that they could go back to work, and they were transferred to other blocks. Some of them even made it home in fairly good shape. Yes, as we shall see, the year 1943 signaled a great change in the camp.

Our ration at Dachau was one-and-a-half loaves of camp bread per person a week, or three to four slices a day, and less than two pints of soup per day—soup which was almost all water. Every week we could count on getting red or white cabbage soup at least five times, carrot or spinach soup once, and macaroni soup every Sunday. There was little or no fat in it, and if you found three sugar-lump-size pieces of meat in your soup in a single week, you could be happy.

With our bread we got about one ounce of butter and one tablespoon of jam a week, plus one slice of soggy bologna and perhaps a half ounce of dry, gritty cheese. Sometimes, instead of coffee, we would get something we called "grunt-soup," a hot, greyish-brown liquid. And every day we could count on getting from three to six unpeeled potatoes of dubious quality.

The camp canteen made all kinds of water-bloated products available at outrageous prices. The beer that was sold, for example, wasn't real beer, but carbonated water with a very queer flavor. It spoiled very quickly. For a long time, also, we almost gassed ourselves on their special sausage, which wasn't sausage at all, but a big tube of ground-up carrots and turnips held together with gelatin to resemble bologna. Such a "sausage" cost us a fortune even though it contained very little food value. Two or three times a year the canteen sold pieces of blood sausage. But the supply wasn't even enough to provide for half a block. Some said that it wasn't even made with real blood.

Once we were poisoned by a shipment of salted oysters that had been condemned for regular consumption. You could smell them from one end of camp to the other. But what do you do when you are voracious, racked by hunger? For days we bought spoiled oysters. Even after they had been rinsed repeatedly, they were almost unbearably salty. Most of us got violently sick, and quite a few died. For ten days I felt more dead than alive. But a couple of weeks later we were back in the canteen again looking for another bargain. We were crazy with hunger. Sometimes raw vegetables were available: carrots, turnips, cabbage, lettuce, and big, tasteless pumpkins.

But decently nourishing food products were never for sale. By 1943 the imitation beer was just about all that was left. That was no tragedy, however, because by that time we were getting all kinds of food packages from outside. The canteen foods were all actually bad for us, except for the bread. We had edematous legs, hands, stomachs, and faces, and the vitiated foods only added more water. But it was hard to resist them because we were not only ravenously hungry, we were also parched with thirst.

To drink water from the taps was extremely dangerous: it was contaminated with dysentery and typhoid germs. Dachau was poorly located because there was peat under the ground, and the wells had not been sunk deep enough, so that the water was polluted. Prisoners who couldn't resist drinking it were called "goners" because it was only a matter of time before they died from dysentery or typhoid. In addition, the climate in Dachau was not very healthful. Nine months of the year we were plagued by the "Foehn" winds—warm, sultry winds that drained all your strength. It was especially hard on people with weak hearts, and many died of strokes during those months. The whole environment was chosen not only to make life as hard as possible, but also to deprive us of all conditions necessary for human life to exist at all.

Besides the blows, beatings, and kicks delivered on the spur of the moment, the camp also had official punishments. Anyone who was caught violating one of the many camp rules, which were read once a week, was sentenced to a special punishment. Many things were forbidden. You could be punished officially for any one of a host of things. I'll mention only a few.

You could be punished if you carried anything more in your pockets than one handkerchief and a piece of toilet paper; in other words, if a letter from home, or a piece of bread, a carrot, a potato, a knife, or anything else were found on you, you were in trouble. Also, if you were loafing during working hours or if you didn't greet an S.S. man quickly or respectfully enough, the guards had it in for you. If you "organized" something outside of our kommando; if you discussed politics; if you failed to fasten the top button on your zebra suit; or if a straw were found out of place on your straw mattress or a stain on your cup or a spot in your storage square—all these "offenses" brought the Nazis' wrath upon you.

Punishment for these offenses could consist of withholding part of your ration for a number of days, or of your being assigned to a penal kommando for several weeks or months. Or you could draw "twenty-five," that is, twenty-five lashes across your buttocks. Everyone dreaded this form of punishment. The lashes were always administered after evening roll call in full view of all prisoners. The sentenced man was stretched out on a wooden horse, with his hands and feet tied. Then two guards took turns beating him with a special cane. The beating inflicted wounds that were severe enough to kill a person. The cane could lay the victim's backside wide open. One of my German colleagues who got "twenty-five" hovered between life and death for fourteen days. He had to spend nine months in the infirmary before he was considered cured. One day about twenty prisoners were given "twenty-five" at one time. Their screams and groans

ONE OF MY GERMAN COLLEAGUES WHO GOT "TWENTY-FIVE"
HOVERED BETWEEN LIFE AND DEATH FOR FOURTEEN DAYS.

echoed and re-echoed between the barracks.

Moreover, anyone officially sentenced could depend on receiving not only a public punishment, but also a hidden punishment. He could plan on getting from six to twelve months added to his original sentence.

In this chapter I have tried to give the reader some idea of what a German concentration camp was like. I must add that, according to reliable prisoners who were in Dachau during the years before my arrival, things were much worse then. They told me stories of incredible, demonic atrocities; but I will relate only what I experienced for myself and what I know to be the truth.

Human Sacrifices to the Goddess "Sauberkeit"

We had reached the train terminal in Dachau. S.S. men and big trucks were waiting to carry us to camp. The transfer was carried out with a generous complement of blows and kicks, and constant screaming: "Los, los! Tempo, tempo, tempo! Auf geht's, auf geht's! Hop, hop, hop!" We were driven around the city of Dachau and eventually arrived at the huge S.S. camp. There we passed through several gates and check points, each of them heavily guarded. It was easy to see that there would be no escaping from this place.

We were unloaded even more violently than we had been loaded; there were no civilians watching here. We were pummeled and thrown out of the trucks. Then we were herded to the administration building to be registered. There, we had to act as reverently as if we were in a religious shrine. Each small impropriety drew a slap in the face. On the wall we could see a system of cards that said much, none of it good. We could see that the prisoners were divided into different categories: there were red, green, black, yellow, purple, pink, and blue cards. Those were the living prisoners—about 15,000 in all.

Off to the side, we saw a very small category titled, "Ent-lassen" (released). To be released, obviously, was very much the exception rather than the rule. Under the heading "Gestorben" (deceased) there was an entire wall filled with cards: death seemed to be the rule. The mute system of cards screamed murder! An S.S. man looked me over and asked me, "And what do *you* do?" When I told him that I was a clergyman, he answered, "Ha! In two weeks you'll celebrate Ascension Day—up through the chimney." Half an hour later, we walked through the main gate of the prison camp, loaded with dark promises.

Next we were taken to the building where our civilian clothing and personal possessions were to be stored. Here we had to surrender all our luggage, even our toilet articles. Whatever looked usable or valuable disappeared into a huge basket under the counter. We all had to strip completely, and our clothes and shoes were put into a paper bag and marked with our prison numbers. We were given a receipt to sign, listing what we had turned in.

Here, too, a semblance of correct order was observed, right to the smallest details. The prisoners (Prominents) working for the S.S. in this building had also adopted the methods of their superiors. Signing the receipt went as follows: Suddenly, without explanation, a paper was thrust under the nose of the new arrival. He was immediately expected to know that he had to sign it, and where, and why. If he did not do so within a couple of seconds, he got a slap in the face. The S.S. slogan was not "Say it with flowers," but "Say it with violence!"

This was their way of whittling people down and hollowing them out. Everything down to the minutiae of their daily existence was aimed at degrading the prisoners, stripping them of their self-respect, and treating them as totally worthless. For example, a few days after our arrival, we had to be registered as a safeguard against escape attempts. A total picture was required: fingerprints, scars, photos in different poses, even our manner of walking was recorded. So we were photographed in various positions, including a sitting position. However, to say, "Finished! You can get up now" was below the S.S. photographer's dignity, so in the seat of the stool he had rigged a little gadget that drove a large needle into your rump right after the camera clicked. You stood up automatically!

After this, stark naked, we had to parade to the showers, where we were also shorn and shaved and issued a set of prison clothes. Camp custom decreed that the newcomers got the very worst clothes and shoes in stock. We were a pitiful spectacle: nervous, frightened, and very uncomfortable in our miserable, ill-fitting rags. Camp underwear was made of blue drill with a white stripe, but it was usually in such poor shape that it was hard to tell the shorts from the shirt. Then came the zebra suit, with blue-grey stripes and a round beret of the same material.

Socks were regarded as superfluous, a luxury. Our shoes consisted of wooden sandals with a strip of cloth over the toes. They slipped off at every step and seemed designed to provide the most discomfort and trouble to our feet and legs. Edema and lesions, ulcers and splitting, had already made most prisoners' feet extremely sore; and their condition was aggravated by the awkward sandals that continually tripped us up. They kept coming off (a punishable offence), and kicked our ankles raw.

The slightest scratch picked up under camp conditions meant doctoring yourself for several months or for the rest of your imprisonment, because every scratch became a festering sore. Before we began receiving food packages, I had several deep sores on my hands and feet that resulted from superficial nicks which initially had not even drawn blood. Many amputations and even deaths could be traced to those murderous sandals.

From the showers, we were marched across the parade square down the main street of the camp to Block 17, the Admission Block. It was not an easy walk, for the street was paved with uneven cobblestones. By now it was 9 P.M. The Admission Block, like the others, consisted of four sitting rooms and four bedrooms, with a bathroom for every four bedrooms. All together there were twelve bathroom sinks, six basins for rinsing feet or shoes, and six toilets.

Taking army barracks as a norm, each combination of sitting room and bedroom could accommodate from thirty to forty men. But in Dachau, the same space held eighty to two-hundred and sometimes close to three-hundred men. In fact, as a result of transfers from other camps, during the last days of the war the number rose to five- or six-hundred men per room. If health standards had been observed, the camp could not have held more than five thousand men at most.

In 1942, however, the camp held twelve thousand men. The total rose to between fifteen and eighteen thousand in 1943. Most blocks became so crowded that three to five and sometimes even seven men had to share two mattresses. No one got very much rest that way. Just prior to liberation, the total number of men in the camp rose to forty or fifty thousand. So conditions became even worse.

Upon our arrival in camp, each of us got a loaf of bread and a couple of pints of sago-soup, actually imitation sago. It was a gelatinous liquid with a few bits of dried vegetable floating in it. The nutritional value was minimal, but it filled our stomachs for a while. Our group was spread over four different rooms. De Geus, Idema, Sietsma, Tunderman, and I were all assigned to Room 2, where Willy Bader, the man I mentioned earlier, was room elder.

The inside of the Administration Block was an unusual sight. We couldn't believe our eyes! Was this place really inhabited by one to two hundred men? In Amersfoort everything had always been a loathsome mess, so that one hesitated to touch anything. But here everything was spic and span, spit and polish. You could literally eat from the floor. There wasn't a nook or cranny anywhere that had not been thoroughly dusted. The windows were so clean that they looked as if the glass had been removed.

The floor was swept at least four times a day and also "blocked" three times a day, that is, washed with large brushes fastened on wooden blocks and then buffed with a block swaddled in rags. Once a week it was also waxed and given an extra good "blocking." Everything in the place was sacred. Nothing existed to serve man, but vice versa: man had to serve these inanimate things. It was idolatry in its most literal sense. The health and strength, peace and comfort, the very lives of the prisoners were sacrificed to this idol of materiality. The normal relationship between people and things was completely reversed.

To have someone spill a drop of water on the immaculate floor was much worse than to have a prisoner die from the strain of "blocking" this holy ground. If a spot were found on one of the aluminum cups, the walls trembled and the windows rattled with the repercussions. You would have thought that someone had been murdered! But when the great goddess *Sauberkeit* (purity) claimed several victims a day through utter exhaustion, it was hardly worth noting.

Every time that we entered the sitting room, even if fifty times a day, we had to remove our sandals, wash both sandals and feet thoroughly and dry them bone-dry before we might reverently enter the sanctuary. Sometimes we got away with whispering, but that too was forbidden. Total silence was the law. We were almost afraid to breathe for fear it would fog up the shine on the highly polished tables.

After our arrival, we were lined up in one corner, where we stood gaping like people entering the hallowed stillness of a Medieval cathedral for the first time. Each of us received a small pan, an aluminum cup and plate, a steel knife and spoon, a towel and a dishrag from the room elder, Willy Bader, and his two Polish helpers. Each item was spotless and shiny. Along the walls of the room stood fifty high, narrow lockers made of soft wood and painted only on the outside.

The next day we were given detailed instructions on how to take care of all these things. After every meal, our utensils had to be taken to the washroom and washed in cold water. Cold water was adequate because the soup contained no fat. Then all the utensils had to be polished with newspaper until they shone like a mirror. Everything had to be in exemplary order because the Admission Block was the model block shown to visiting Red Cross officials to demonstrate to them the hygienic conditions maintained in the camp. This obsession with hygiene went to such an extreme, that it claimed many lives.

The word *sauberkeit* (purity) was repeated hundreds of times a day. Each of us was issued a piece of sandpaper to scour the inside of our lockers, so that the raw wood was spotless. Everything was inspected twice a day, and pity the man whose things were not *sauber*. The windows were cleaned twice a day so that even the flies had no chance to dirty the glass.

Our room elder, Willy Bader, wasn't bad compared to his counterparts in the other barracks. They not only saw to it that things were kept in exemplary order, but they were tyrannical and vicious in their treatment of the prisoners. They beat and kicked the men, nor did they allow them the rest that they officially had a right to. Our room elder was meticulously fair in his strictness, however. He never assigned work just to torment us or tire us out. Only what was strictly necessary had to be done—but that had to be done perfectly!

He possessed an uncanny knowledge of human character, and it did not take him long to classify newcomers: they were either *anstaendige Leute* (decent men) or *Schuften und Lumpen* (bums and good-for-nothings). He was generally able to weed out the riff-raff, the egocentrics, and the criminals. To be assigned to his room was a great advantage.

The mortality rate was considerably lower under his regimen than under the other room elders. This, however, made his position difficult and precarious. He had been in the camp since 1933, so he had been one of the few to survive the first years of extreme hardship and had thereby earned the job of room elder. He was able to keep this job without beating anyone because he had a knack for getting through touchy situations and because he was always on top of things. He was instrumental in saving not only my life but also that of Rev. Idema, the only one of my colleagues to survive. And there were many others whom he similarly preserved from death. Had we been assigned to one of the other rooms, we would have been in much worse physical shape when we went to work in one of the kommandos. We would never have made it, for toward the end, even then, we were both on the verge of death.

Our whole day consisted of training: we learned *Sauberkeit*; we learned to sing S.S. songs and to march; we learned to distinguish the various S.S. ranks; we learned how to report to the doctor, who, however, was never available, and the commandant, who was inaccessible, and to every other S.S. rank. You marched up to the man, whipped off your cap, snapped to attention, and announced in a loud voice: "Schutzhaeftling Overduin, Hollaender, 30650, meldet sich gehorsamst zur stelle" (Prisoner Overduin, Dutchman, 30650, reporting here as ordered). Slow learners ended up standing outside in the rain, the heat, or the cold—standing until their trembling legs were swollen and aching.

The day after our arrival, Bader selected Idema and me to be his helpers—a tremendous privilege. He was a very emphatic, dedicated anticlerical. But even though he knew that we were clergymen, this did not stop him from choosing us. We did our best to live up to his expectations, but we were no match for the two Poles. The latter were much stronger, for they had made contacts that gave them access to extra food.

"Blocking" the floor was particularly excruciating work. Whenever Bader noticed that we were unable to go on, he would take over and do our work. The gulf between a room elder and a prisoner was infinite. A room elder held the power of life and death over a prisoner. He could protect you or turn you over to the S.S. for punishment, which often meant a speedy death. He could make so many demands on you that you couldn't possibly last more than a few days. There were prisoners who arrived healthy and well-nourished, but who expired in two weeks or less. Ailments that otherwise would never have prevented a person from leading a normal life and living to an old age now caused the deaths of many prisoners because of the unconscionable demands that their bodies and nervous systems were subjected to.

After blocking the floor, we had to wash the windows. This was light work, so we stretched it out to three or four hours. It helped us to conserve our strength. We thanked God for our privileged position again and again. As helpers we got a little extra food—a potato or a ladle full of soup—almost every day, and it was always received as an answer to prayer. But our hearts plummeted each time the summons came, "Food-carriers out!"

Three times a day we had to go and pick up the enormous kettles of coffee or soup from the kitchen. The kettles were made of steel with double walls and a heavy lid; when filled with coffee or soup, they weighed well over two hundred pounds. Six hundred men converged on the kitchen to pick up three hundred full kettles and lug them to the barracks. We marched to the kitchen praying for strength. In the huge kitchen, which we had to enter reverently, hat in hand, stood several rows of kettles flanked by S.S. guards who hurried us along. Idema and I seized the kettle by its steel handles and summoned all our strength. But we could hardly lift the thing off the ground. We were too weak.

Before we could get moving, an S.S. man was beating on us. "Tempo, tempo! Los, los!" It was obedience or death. The hot soup slopped over our hands. We were out of the kitchen.

"Set it down," I gasped, "or I'll drop it." There we stood panting. On the street the block elders and S.S. men awaited us. They moved between the food-carriers shouting, kicking, and dealing out blows. "Auf geht's! Los, los!" (Lets go! Hustle, hustle!)

Ten steps. Twenty. Scalded hands and feet. Stop and rest. Driven on again. Stumble on, step . . . by . . . step . . . . The parade ground seemed endless. Then the main street. Stretching on and on. How many had failed to make it? How

HOW MANY HAD LOST THEIR LIVES ON THIS
SOUP-RUN?

many had lost their lives on this soup-run? But this terrible task provided us with many wonderful memories as well as fearful ones. The whole route was one continuous prayer. And we thanked God from the depths of our hearts when we had made it once again, or when we drew a kettle with a low number so that the soup-run was shorter.

But what a shattering disappointment it was when, just as we thought we were finished, we were sent back for another kettle! There was always the danger that the scalding soup would cause suppurating sores which could cause you to be declared unfit and sent to the Invalid Block. This could mean a quick and miserable end.

For Idema and me, the six weeks in the Admission Block were unforgettably beautiful as to our spiritual life. We became so closely bound up with each other that we were often confused with one another. Everywhere we saw the hand of God. Every day we experienced answers to prayer. Together we bore the suffering, we shared the blows, and together we recited one Psalm after another as we polished the windows.

Hunger pains tormented us constantly; the days seemed infinitely long, and our soup ration infinitely small and watery. In the first months we had not yet built up any credit, so we couldn't buy anything extra. One day, however, we were unexpectedly favored. Our room elder gave us each a large radish. We were elated! We made the two of them last three days as a supplement to our regular ration, by cutting each one into six slices, which we ate between mealtimes. At 9:30 in the morning and at 4:00 in the afternoon we each took one slice to quiet the constant gnawing in our bellies.

Another thing that we had to learn was making beds. We spent hours and days learning to do this properly. The mattress first had to be stuffed with straw through a large opening at the top. Then the straw had to be distributed perfectly, evenly, so that no lumps or hollows showed. The mattress had to be as smooth as a table top. We learned to pack and poke with a stick until the mattress had square corners all around, so that it looked like a box, especially when it was meticulously and tightly wrapped in a sheet.

The pillow, too, had to be made as square as a box and just as hard. The spread had to be folded exactly to one-third size to cover the width of the bed and the pillow. Another blanket had to be arranged underneath it so that it was completely invisible. What terrible aggravation and misery this sacrament of bed-making caused us! Heavy penalties were meted out if it was not done perfectly, and it seldom was. It may sound incredible, but bed-making claimed hundreds, perhaps thousands, of lives in the camp. People died not only of beatings, but they also died from making beds. Of course, it was everything taken together that brought death. Every detail of camp life was designed to require the impossible and to permit less than minimal nourishment and rest.

With his ten years of experience, Willy Bader could point out the "goners" a few days after their arrival. They died in one to four weeks—sometimes eight weeks—after they arrived. My dear friend, Rev. J. De Geus, with whom I had shared so much—good and bad—died in only ten days. Thank God, he was assigned to the same room as we so that we could care for him as much as possible. But camp life put too great a demand on his depleted strength. He longed for death. An hour before he died, he told us, "I long for rest, eternal rest. I would far rather go and be with Christ."

Although we were grateful that God had prepared his way into His eternal Kingdom, we were deeply disturbed and grieved. After only ten days Dachau had claimed the first of our group. Who would be next? A few days later Rev. J. Kapteyn followed. He had already become convinced when we were still in Amersfoort that he would never get out of prison alive, and he lived by the thought of Christ's return. In His eternal wisdom God gave each of us the grace that we needed. The one received the grace to continue to live in Dachau's torment without succumbing spiritually and morally, and the other received the grace to die. Had the Lord not loosed us all from wife and children, family and friends?

One day, in the shower room, Prof. Titus Brandsma suddenly thrust his last pouch of tobacco at me. "Here, take it! You'll be able to make good use of it." His body was used up and disintegrating. Except for his fluid-filled legs, he was reduced to skin and bone. But his spirit was unbroken, and he was always friendly and cheerful in the Lord. It was the last time that I saw him. He had been carrying out his last will and testament. A few days later Titus Brandsma was delivered from the hell of Dachau and transported to heaven. He already had a foretaste of heaven in his heart while he lived in the infernal horrors of Dachau. In Amersfoort he had written the beautiful words:

> Jesus, the mere thought of You
> makes my heart's love ascend
> on the love that streams from You
> and claims me as Your friend.
>
> Although my courage may be tried
> I'll take what life may bring:
> it is the road that You once walked—
> and leads me to my King.
>
> I count all my suffering good,
> acknowledge nothing untoward;
> for all the buffetings of life
> combine to bind me to my Lord.
>
> Plucked out of life and planted here
> in loneliness and pain,
> and far from family and friends,
> I sing no sad refrain.
>
> For You, Lord Jesus, are close by
> in all my pain You have been nigh:
> Stay near, near to me, Jesus dear,
> for life is good when you are here.

Every day anew brought us such signs of grace. Calvin,

too, speaks of the sorrow of the Christian as being mingled with a wonderful joy. So it was with us: suffering, indescribable suffering, yet joy, inexpressable joy. "I count all of my suffering good, acknowledge nothing untoward; for all the buffetings of life combine to bind me to my Lord." Nowhere did we experience heaven's nearness as powerfully as in this anteroom to hell. "Death where is your sting, and hell your victory?" The demonic desolation of the concentration camps could not touch God's children inwardly. In great need, God grants a great measure of His grace.

Again it was with a mixture of discouragement and thankfulness that we gathered around the body of another colleague, Dr. K. Sietsma. He died six weeks after our arrival. We had benefited greatly from his leadership in our discussions about Biblical principles for human relationships and organizations, and also from his sermons and prayers. His intellect and character and all his gifts were devoted to the service of God. More deaths followed in those first weeks: Rev. Zwiep, whom we all loved for his noble demeanor; and Rev. W. Tunderman, who had been admitted to the infirmary.

Although the deaths of all our fellow prisoners affected us, the deaths among the small Dutch colony—with whom we had been one in the common struggle against compromise and death—hit us hardest. Yet, if they died at peace with God, we grieved not for them, but for those they left behind. And we prayed that to them, too, God would show Himself a Father of miraculous comfort, even as He had to those who died in the camp.

Room elder Bader told us time and again, "You fellows think you've got it bad now. Just wait till you get to Block 28 or 30. That's where hell really begins! Those two blocks are the worst ones in the whole camp. The block and room elders there are real devils. No one gets a minute's rest all day. You barely have time to catch your breath. You'll be hounded from 3:30 in the morning until 9 or 10 at night. Beatings are the rule rather than the exception. Because you're a preacher, all your rights will be taken away, and you'll be put in the roughest work kommandos. Prisoners there fall like flies!"

It was a distressingly bleak picture that he painted for us. But we could see it with our own eyes at roll call. All of us—dead-tired, starved, with swollen legs and faces—were a pitiful, macabre sight. In comparison to the men of Blocks 28 and 30, however, we looked pretty good. The residents of those two blocks were all "goners." Only a few hours, days, or weeks, separated them from the crematorium.

We shuddered at the thought of being transferred from the Admission Block to 28 or 30. But the day would come. One day soon we would have to move on because new prisoners were arriving every day. Normally, initiation lasted from one to two weeks. This was usually an automatic thing regulated by the Labor Pool. But Bader managed to keep Idema and me with him for seven weeks. This was a great blessing to us and an answer to prayer. Nevertheless, our strength was diminishing badly.

First we suffered from numb, cold feet—the feared prelude to swollen legs. Then followed the prickling sensation. One dismal morning, we awoke with puffy faces and blisters under our eyes. Then came "pillow hands" and "elephant legs" as our limbs filled with fluid.

We had matriculated to the rank of "goners."

This was the condition that we were in when the awful day arrived that we were transferred to the work blocks. We were ordered to pack up our things. In our seven weeks with Willy Bader, we had managed to organize quite a few things. A few old rags to protect our feet from those clumsy sandals, for example, were tremendous prizes. The transfer took place in early August of 1942. All the non-German clergy went to Block 28. We arrived in a crowded madhouse ruled by the criminally insane.

Death Lurks in Every Corner

The block elder of the Admission Block had introduced us to the secrets of Dachau upon our arrival. In a low voice he had hissed, "Death lurks in every corner!" You don't "pass away" in Dachau, he had told us—you die like a dog! Much of what we experienced in our first seven weeks confirmed his words. But we didn't really understand the ominous, grisly words of the elder until we arrived in Block 28.

We mustered in the street between the blocks to meet our new block elder. He was built like a bull, huge and heavy, with a pink, corpulent face, and eyes that rolled frantically in their sockets. He ranted so furiously, we feared—or perhaps hoped that he would have a stroke. We were not aware of having done anything wrong, but he scolded and screamed at us with such fury that we began to wonder if, perhaps, we were guilty of some major crime we had overlooked. It was a remarkable performance: he worked himself into such a rage that he convinced himself there was a reason for his anger. And every other sentence ended with the threat: "That I guarantee you, sure as hell!"

There is an old saying, "When you want to go crazy, you can't," but this man and three of his room elders were excep-

158

tions. (Incredibly, the fourth room elder was still sane and decent.) The others were able to transform themselves into raving lunatics at any moment, night or day. All they needed to start an abusive diatribe was to catch sight of one of the clergymen from their block. And as they were constantly surrounded by clergymen, they were in a continuous state of turmoil day and night.

We were assigned to Room 3, the roost of the maddest of these madmen. His arbitrariness reminded me of an ancient oriental despot gone berserk! Everyone who displeased him, for any one of a dozen trivial reasons, he beat or killed. Often asking him a necessary question, or just asking him for *permission* to ask a question, was the occasion of a thrashing.

Ironically, he was a fellow prisoner, as were all his room elder colleagues. The block elder was an ex-S.S. man who had been sentenced to prison. Even in the eyes of the S.S. thugs, he was a thug. The other elders were communists. The supreme commandant of the camp considered the only good clergyman to be a dead one, so he had put the worst sadists in command of Blocks 28 and 30.

The first thing that our room elder did was "check" our personal possessions. That is, he confiscated everything he could use and made us throw all that was left into the garbage. Our needle and thread, our bandages, the rags for our feet—everything we had painstakingly "organized" was gone. This ceremony was accompanied by repeated blows and kicks. Apparently to have collected so much was a horrendous offense.

Once settled in Block 28, we soon found that a typical day would begin when we were roused at about 3:30 A.M. with a loud shout: "Aufstehen!" (Get up!). This was the signal for the beginning of a day-long assault on our nerves and bodily strength. We were expected to be out of our bunks in a single bound, even before the shout had died out. And so, daily, the rushing and straining began. At most, we were allowed five hours sleep, but at 3:30, there was no opportunity for yawning or stretching. With faces distorted by anxiety, we would all race around, attempting to get an impossible amount done in a very short time.

The bunks were three high, so there was almost no room to do a decent job of bedmaking. Those who slept in the middle bunks stampeded to the washroom first in order to find a place among the several hundred bodies converging on the twelve wash basins to give their hands, faces, and upper bodies a quick dabbing. Then it would be back to the lockers at a breathless trot to dress, and to fold up towels as specified. If a towel were not folded exactly right, it meant severe punishment at noon. Those who slept on the top and bottom bunks had to be finished with making their beds by this time so that they could hasten to the washroom while the "middlers" worried and shaped their mattresses according to instructions.

To square up a straw mattress perfectly in a few minutes was, of course, impossible. But it had to be done. Our hearts skipped a beat whenever the shout "Kaffee fassen!" (Get your coffee) rang out.

Hurry, hurry! When we heard "Kaffee fassen!", we were expected to drop everything, scramble to our place in line by our locker, and stand ready with a little pan to march by the room elder for a pint of coffee. This seldom happened without incident. One man would hold his pan too close, and another too far away; another was holding his pan crookedly, and still another was too slow or too pushy. Whatever the offense, it demanded a punch in the face. We had to drink the gritty liquid while we were standing up (sometimes it was "grunt soup," a brown liquid with a little flour stirred in). If we did not have the self-discipline to save a piece of bread from the previous evening's meal (and most didn't), this liquid was all that we had for breakfast.

We were permitted to stand still for a few minutes to down our breakfasts; the room elder would use this occasion to go charging about, dealing out punishments for offenses that he had spied while we were dressing and making our beds. Then, once again, we would join the mob in the washroom to rinse our pans. By this time, several of the prisoners might have black eyes, bloody noses, and other fresh cuts and bruises.

From the washroom, it was back to the lockers, to scour our utensils until they shone and to sand the insides of our lockers. As we worked, a thunderstorm of threats and curses would roll over our heads and backs. We were continuously reminded what penalties awaited us should our bedmaking and cleaning not be up to standard.

"This place is a pigpen!" the room elder would roar. "Today you're gonna wish you'd never been born, I guarantee you!" (He was always willing to guarantee everything that he said.)

We would work on in deathly silence. Our desperate labors were broken off only by the command "Raus!" Anyone who didn't immediately pack everything away, jump into his sandals, and line up outside, cap in hand, was pummeled and kicked outside. A few men always stayed behind to sweep and dust the bedroom and to mop out the sitting room, washroom and toilets. We took turns at this duty, working in groups of twenty men.

Outside in the darkness of early dawn we often had to wait a full ten minutes before the order came to fall in. We'd line up in a formation of about 600 men; the tallest in front and the shortest to the rear. All other work blocks lined up at the same time. When the whistle or siren blew we marched ten abreast, to the parade ground. The room elders and the block elder looked us over, searching for any irregularities, while one man kept the rhythm: "Left, two, three, four. Left. Left. Left and left."

Along the main street, and on the parade ground the electric lights and the large spotlights were still burning. Daylight had not arrived, yet everyone was dragging already. In the hour we had been up, we had done more than we would normally have done in twice the time at our usual paces. Our nerves were taxed to the breaking point. We never had a chance to relax; and we were racked with hunger. But the day was only beginning—a day of heavy labor and more humiliations.

Each block would march to its appointed spot on the parade ground. Lining up block by block took from fifteen minutes to a half-hour. Everything had to be perfect. The rows of each block had to be perfectly aligned with those of the neighboring blocks. Then, after the well known order, "Attention! Caps off! Eyes left!" had been given and the block bookkeepers had checked the totals, a shout would ring out over the parade ground. "Form your work kommandos!"

Suddenly, thousands of men would begin milling about, pushing and running in every direction. New groups had to be formed, not according to blocks this time, but according to the work kommando to which one had been assigned. However, not everyone was physically capable of competing in this rush. Dying of starvation, swollen legs rotting away, some could only stumble ahead. A few of the men would fall and be unable to go on. They would stay on the ground, hoping for a quick death in the infirmary. But this was easier said than done.

The S.S. operated on the assumption that everyone was faking illness because of inherent laziness, so the stragglers were kicked or dragged to join their work kommandos. Any prisoners who passed out were revived with pails of cold water. According to the S.S., everyone was fit to work. Orders are orders, and in a concentration camp, you are either alive or dead. The living work. Only the dead rest.

An hour later, about 5:30 in the morning, the parade ground would be empty once again. All the kommandos had been read off by the work leader and his staff. They had marched off to the cheerful sound of the S.S. songs they learned at admission. The kommandos varied greatly in size—some as small as three men to those comprising more than fifteen thousand men. Most of them numbered from a few dozen to several hundred men.

The largest kommandos were the Garden Kommando, the Liebhof Kommando, the Factory Kommando, and the Shipping Kommando. The Garden Kommando cared for the huge gardens planted with vegetables, potatoes, and medicinal herbs close by the camp. The Liebhof Kommando cultivated the kitchen gardens and did other farming. It was referred to as the "Friedhof" (cemetery) Kommando. The Factory Kommandos worked in the cannery, in the porcelain factory, or in the munitions and weapons factories. The loading and unloading at the railway docks and in the huge storage yards was done by the Shipping Kommando. Clergymen were generally assigned to the most difficult and dangerous kommandos. Because they were designated as "heavy-labor kommandos," once a day or several times a week prisoners in these kommandos received extra rations; that is, all the prisoners except clergymen.

My first kommando was the Garage Maintenance Kommando—one of the heaviest ones. But it did not get extra rations, for it included only twenty to forty men. Officially, our task was to clean garages, but we never did. We became a kind of miscellaneous kommando. The first week that I was assigned to it, we swept streets, pulled grass from between cobble stones, picked up litter, and removed tree stumps. The second week, we put up hay on the farm of one of the S.S. officers. From the third to the eighth weeks, we unloaded coal cars. We had to pull the cars into the sweltering-hot switching yard by hand. The work was murderous!

By 6 o'clock every morning we had usually reached our destination and collected our tools—shovels, hoes, or axes, from a large storage chest. We would work until 11:30; then we would march back to camp at a quick pace. Officially, we now had the right to about an hour of rest, and our bodies cried out for it—even if it were only a few minutes to sit or lie on the ground. We would have traded kingdoms for a short nap and the whole world for a solid meal. But, instead, we would trot from the parade ground to our block with a knot of fear in our stomach. What would await us there?

One look inside would be enough to confirm our worst fears. Instead of an hour of rest, we would find that we were in for an hour of fun and games in the devil's playhouse. All our mattresses, blankets, and sheets had usually been flung out, forming a huge heap in the middle of the room; and everything had been covered by a thick layer of dust that had come out of the straw mattresses.

While we had been busy expending more energy than we thought we had, our room elder's sadistic brain had also been busy. We were famished and longing for a little soup and a minute of rest, but our elder had found a straw from one of the mattresses on the floor and had devised a new form of collective punishment. No one might have any soup until the barracks were in perfect order.

We would frantically wash our shoes, feet, and hands and rush into the bedroom, where we would be welcomed with curses and blows. We would then go to work rebuilding our straw mattresses and remaking our beds, toiling like madmen. After three quarters of an hour of frantic labor, anxious lest we miss our soup, we would be done. We could line up to get our soup.

But we would no sooner swallow the first few spoonsful, when the flushed, bullish head of the block elder would appear in the doorway. He would bellow in righteous outrage! He had heard that we had made an absolute sty of our bedroom. Uttering an incoherent stream of curses, he would grab a broomstick and attack us all in a fit of rage. Chasing us into a corner of the barracks, he would belabor our heads and shoulders with his broomstick as if he were demon-possessed.

"Pigs! All you can do is eat like pigs! But you're all too lazy to work! Out of here! Out! Out! Out!" And he would beat us right out of our block. He would force us to dump our soup into the toilets and rinse, clean, and store away our small pans, and all the while our apoplectic block elder would be bellowing, "Fall in, fall in!" And then we would be marched back to the parade ground.

Ahead of us lay six and a half hours of hard labor under the scorching sun. How were we going to make it through the afternoon? Praying for strength, we would force our bodies

PIGS! ALL YOU CAN DO IS EAT LIKE PIGS!

on. And soon we would be back in the coal cars, shoveling coal into large sacks that weighed well over a hundred pounds each when filled. These sacks had to be loaded onto a truck, and then ten or twelve of us had to pull the truck by hand to the coal bins or to the officers' quarters. Either trip took almost an hour of superhuman effort.

We would haul at the heavy trucks like emaciated galley slaves. Four men would pull from the front and two other groups of four would pull on ropes attached to the sides of the truck. A foreman or S.S. man would repeatedly test the ropes for tautness to see whether we were pulling hard enough. A flurry of blows and kicks would mean that we weren't. Back and forth we hauled the truck.

Exhausted, we kept collapsing under the weight of the coal sacks as we loaded the truck. Each time it seemed that it would be impossible to lift another sack onto our shoulder. But some young S.S. guard would beat on our backs and heads until the impossible somehow became possible.

Once I had to ask one of the officers' wives whether the coal was to be brought in through the basement window or through the upstairs. The woman was already down in the basement. When I put my head through the basement window to ask her, she let out a piercing scream and fled, for when she looked up and saw me, her face filled with terror. I hadn't realized how horrible I looked. My face was that of the Wandering Jew. I was down to forty kilograms (85 lbs.)—a living skeleton. And the coal dust made me look even more like a fleshless skull come to life. I told myself, "Careful! Stay calm. So what if you look like death itself? By God's grace you'll make it. One day you'll look back at this and laugh!" For someone in my condition, to lose courage meant death.

Miraculously, we somehow made it through the day. We would be marched, double time, back to the parade ground, and there further torment would await us. We thronged together, a wretched, bruised mass. Some of us would be carrying dead or dying comrades, for even the dead had to participate in the evening roll call. Otherwise the numbers wouldn't tally, and that would be much more serious than the mere loss of another life.

The evening ceremonies would usually last from an hour and a half to two hours—our reward for an interminable day of excruciating labor. We would be endlessly aligned until we stood in perfect rows. The block bookkeepers would count their blocks, and then we would all wait until his royal highness, the commandant, arrived, having taken a leisurely time to review the reports. Often he would still be finishing his supper or just visiting and making small talk with his staff, while, outside thousands of prisoners stood waiting for him, either cursing him in their abysmal misery or praying for mercy to endure.

It was indeed a time for curses or prayers, and sometimes for both at the same time.

On some days, roll call would be our only opportunity to stand still, eyes closed, and have communion with our Supreme Commandant, Jesus Christ. Blocks 26, 28, and 30 were all united in prayer. My friend and colleague next to me would elbow me and whisper, "It's all clear!" This was the signal we would use to join together in singing silently, in our hearts, the evensong:

> I lift my praise
> to You, my God most high.
> The sun's last rays
> fade from the evening sky;
> but not Your Light—
> Your Light will never die.
> You make my darkness bright
> when You're nearby.
>
> When darkness falls
> and roads are hard to see,
> Your sweet voice calls
> a welcome out to me;
> and like a father,

reaching lovingly,
You, Lord, will gather
us eternally.

This is the secret of faith: to be able to thank God for His grace and for His fatherly love in the worst of circumstances, even after a day in which you have been deprived of everything necessary for life.

You may say, "That's absurd!" And it is, to those who look for life's secret in external well-being. But to those who know of another, a spiritual world, the Kingdom of God, this secret of thankfulness has been revealed. Didn't Christ say, "I thank thee Father that thou hast hidden these things from the wise and understanding (wise in their own eyes and living only by mortal sight) and revealed them to babes." Those who are citizens of the Kingdom of Heaven are convinced that, although they may know what is *pleasing* to them, they do not always know what is *good* for them. This only their heavenly Father can know.

Faith says that everything which happens to us will be turned to our good by our Father, and will serve our eternal salvation. In other words, in the Kingdom of God, we learn to think differently about what is good for us. We are even able to derive spiritual profit from mistreatment. But at the same time, the villains who cause such misery are responsible for their deeds, and justice demands that they be punished. The question is, do we have an eye, not just for the brutalities that call for divine retribution, but also for the gracious sovereignty of God that enables His children to experience those brutalities in such a way that it is to their spiritual and eternal profit.

Like all suffering caused by injustice, the drama of the concentration camp had a human and a divine side. Those who saw only the human side either went berserk with vengeance or drowned in misery. Those who saw only the divine side could not comprehend God's justice, which is executed on earth also through and by men. But I was describing an average day in Block 28.

The exhausting evening roll call lasted for an hour to an hour and a half. Finally, would come the welcome words, "Prisoners, attention! Eyes left!" In respectful silence, the reports would be taken to the commandant. Then block by block, we would receive the order, "Block 28, about face!" and we would march to our blocks singing "Die Blaue Dragonen," "Silesienland, O Heimatland," or some other nonsense song. We had to sing, loud and strong, but we couldn't. We could only gasp for air, we were so exhausted. I could move my lips, but no sound would come, I was so completely spent. Many others would be similarly voiceless. This only infuriated the block elder, so he would devise more exercises for our punishment.

By this time it would be nearing 9 o'clock. Our throats and stomachs were aching for a cup of coffee and a piece of bread, and our bodies longed for our mattresses. But even when we had reached our block, we still had to remain standing at attention. Flanked by four room elders, our block elder would once again go into one of his terrible tirades. His eyes would roll ominously as he worked himself into a screaming, slathering delirium. The outcome would be a half hour of quick marching up and down in front of our block. We were convinced that we couldn't go another step. But we did! From 3:15 in the morning until 9 o'clock at night, we would not have had a moment's rest, and we would have eaten almost nothing. We entered our barracks more dead than alive.

By this time it would be too late to eat, because too many other things had to be done. Everyone had to crowd about the washrooms and toilets; before entering the sleeping quarters, we had to wash our feet and upper bodies and also rinse and grease our shoes. And, as I have said, there were only a few sinks. This was another way they had of taxing our nerves to the breaking point. We were allowed only a few minutes to perform these tasks, and there was simply not enough room for 300 people in the bathroom. Nor were there enough taps or brushes or grease. The bodily pressure turned us into a brawling, clawing mass. It was absolutely impossible for us to be finished in the allotted time, and this would provide the block elder with further excuse to lash into us for laziness and sabotage.

Finally, we would receive our coffee, bread, and the rest of our ration for the day. The first evening I was in the block, we had coffee, a little butter, and a few unpeeled potatoes—a great meal by usual camp standards! But it was not to be a regular occurrence. Our meals soon turned into melees, for after the food was dished out, we would not be given a minute's time to eat it.

What could we do with our food in so short a time? Saving it in our lockers overnight was forbidden. So was taking it to our bunks to eat it there. But we would have no time to eat it then. So we were clearly deprived of the basic conditions that make life possible. We had to be very resourceful to devise some way to save our precious bits of food in that mad stampede.

Those of us who didn't react quickly in such intolerable situations suffered severely, for these conditions occurred again and again. These same prisoners also attracted most of the beatings. Many could not respond quickly because they were dull and lifeless; they were no longer in control of their nerves, and they were helpless under stress. They would look about with frantic, witless eyes, like spooked animals.

At the door to our sleeping quarters the room elder would check everyone. First, we had to undress in our living quarters. No part of our uniforms could be used to keep us warm at night. We were also checked to see whether we had smuggled food or anything else into our beds and to ensure that our feet were spotless. I usually managed to get my feet washed after a fashion, but many others never got the chance. Besides, with everyone cleaning their shoes in the washroom, it became such a muddy mess that to get out of there with clean feet was almost impossible even if you *had* washed them. Therefore, we could usually count on a couple of punches in the head when we got to the bedroom door.

When I lifted my feet that first night to show them to that priest of satan, disaster struck. The piece of bread that I had concealed in my underwear slipped to the floor right in front of the room elder. He started kicking me like a madman, but that didn't stop me from snatching up my bread and dashing for my bunk. I thanked God that he couldn't follow (right behind me were more offenders who had to be dealt with). Meanwhile, up on my bunk on the second level, I quietly devoured my potatoes, bread and butter. I had run the gauntlet; I had made it through the day.

Soon the room would grow quiet, except for the snoring of the men. Many would pass into a stupor of sleep the moment that they hit their mattress. In our living room, the elder still clattered about. He would check the shoe racks. Everyone had to put his clogs in a numbered spot, so when the room elder made his check to see whether all the shoes had been cleaned and greased, he could easily pick out the offenders.

After about half an hour, he would be finished with his check. Our sadistic supervisor was certain to find some other excuse to crack heads. Like a furious demon, he would burst into the bedroom, yelling to wake the sleeping men and execrate them for being a bunch of filthy, stinking swine. The numbers of the offending persons were read off, and they would have to get out of their beds and go forward for a beating.

If the room elder were in a good mood, he would postpone the beating until first thing in the morning. But before leaving, he would announce that the flagrant offences would be reported to the S.S. He was going to put a stop to them once and for all, he promised. So the poor wretches would have more punishment to look forward to.

What would it be? A beating with a club? Several weeks or months of short rations? Assignment to a penal kommando that would drain them of their last strength? This was how room would be made for newcomers into Blocks 28 and 30; this was how house cleaning was done, and this was how hundreds of clergymen celebrated Ascension Day—up through the chimney.

The block elder in the Admission Block was right: death lurked in every corner. It was not that all the prisoners were eventually beaten to death, although this did happen on occasion, but every aspect of life in our block was designed to bring about the dissolution of life. Whether we were making our beds, washing our feet, carrying the ponderous soup containers, working on a coal kommando, standing at roll call, singing or marching, cleaning our shoes or collecting our bread ration, the design of debilitation and programmed attrition was evident and inexorable.

Finally, a genuine stillness would settle over the room. It would usually happen somewhere between 11 and 11:30 P.M. The thought that in about four hours the whole thing would begin all over again was enough to fill our hearts with dread and despair. So soon a voice would be yelling, "Aufstehen!" and the ungodly torture would start again—the beginning of another endless, murderous day.

Thus the days followed one another—seven days a week, thirty days a month. Each day was another day of fear and suffering, day after day, week after week, month after month. Even Sunday brought no relief. Sundays were no different from the other days of the week.

My description of a typical day in Block 28 was drawn largely from my first day there. I realized that I had landed in an organized madhouse, among the criminally insane, and that not only were the patients in charge, but that they had been given unlimited power. The following days went much like the first, better in some respects, worse in others. For weeks, we never once got a chance just to sit down and relax. We rushed from 3:30 in the morning until about 9:30 at night without being able to sit or lie down. During our half-hour break from 12:30 to 1 o'clock, we would stand in front of our block, for to sit on the ground was a punishable offense. It was considered sabotage and was subject to collective and personal punishment.

During August and September, my job in the heavy-work kommando became unbearable. My weight was forty kilograms (85 lbs.), and my legs and hands were swollen with fluid. My body was covered with lesions, holes caused by starvation. My back was criss-crossed by bloody furrows. With no flesh to cushion the sacks of coal that I had to carry, the burlap rubbed raw my ribs and bones and broke the skin across my back. My kidneys were also starting to bleed, and I vomited blood almost every day.

Starvation was also beginning to affect my memory. Greetings that my wife passed on to me from friends and family were a cause of grief, for I could no longer remember who they were. Slowly, agonizingly, my body was beginning to disintegrate. Perhaps I should say, *quickly* and painfully, because many perished in only a few days or weeks.

The end of October and the beginning of November was my low point. The coal kommando had become unbearable; not just because I expected to collapse completely at any time, but also because we had a demented subforeman. He seemed committed to working me, the only clergyman in that group, to death as efficiently as possible.

As soon as he discovered that I was a clergyman, the foreman made life impossible for me. He assured me, "I'll be done with you in three days, you holy hypocrite, you miserable pile of manure! That's all it takes: three days to break the likes of you!" And, indeed, he did his best to break me in three days. Whenever we marched to the coal trucks, he walked right behind me, repeatedly kicking my legs and feet. More and more lesions were opened in my fluid-filled legs, running sores that could prove fatal after a time.

He also gave me the heaviest jobs. And he always made sure that my coal sacks were filled to the top. When we were loading the trucks, I was made to load ten sacks while everyone else loaded five. I never worked fast enough to suit him. The man also assaulted me directly, beating and kicking me bloody in fits of unrestrained hatred, for my alleged laziness. His dirty work was always accompanied by

WOULD I PERISH UNDER THE
HEAVY LOADS AND ABUSE IN THE
COAL KOMMANDO?

outrageous curses. I was also systematically excluded from the group. For example, when our kommando had "organized" a little extra soup from the S.S. kitchen, everyone else sat down and enjoyed himself while I was forced to work on with nothing to eat. The sub-foreman was determined to destroy me.

I was then most intensely aware of what Jesus went through for me, yet God's Holy Spirit was with me in Dachau. Battered and beaten down like a piece of garbage, I was still able to sing in my heart:

> Lord, though I walk in troubles sore,
> Thou wilt restore my faltering spirit;
> Though angry foes my soul alarm,
> Thy mighty arm will save and cheer it.
> Yea, Thou wilt finish perfectly
> What Thou for me hast undertaken;
> May not Thy works, in mercy wrought,
> E'er come to naught or be forsaken.

Even if in our external circumstances we are wretched, in spirit we are still the most blessed people on earth if we can sing these words. After hellish days, and after hellish roll calls, and hellish receptions at the barracks, it was a miracle that I was still breathing and that my heart was still beating. Then I would repeat the words of St. Paul, "He delivered us from so deadly a peril, and he will deliver us; on him we have set our hope that he will deliver us again" (II Cor. 1:10).

Meanwhile, I knew that I had to get out of the coal kommando; otherwise, I would surely perish under the heavy loads and the relentless abuse. But how? I could expect nothing from the Labor Pool, for it was run by the communists, and their policy was to give the worst jobs to the clergy. Officially there was a directive on the books that those who were weak should be assigned to the lighter kommandos. But who paid any attention to such lenient directives—or to clergymen? Pastors and priests had no contact at all with the Labor Pool.

Moreover, our block was isolated. In our non-existent "free time," we were not allowed to leave our street to visit the other blocks or any of the other facilities. Therefore, I took the hopelessness of my situation to the Lord, and I asked Him to deliver me from that murderous kommando. My friend and colleague Idema also spent one week in this kommando but, thank God, he was transferred to another one. Another friend of mine, Arnold Van Lierop, a Roman Catholic priest, had died in my kommando even before that fiendish subforeman joined it. His death caused Hinloopen, Idema, and me profound grief because he had become our intimate friend. We had shared a locker, slept next to each other, and worked side by side in the coal kommando. Before we went to sleep each night, we said good night to one another with a text from Scripture. Van Lierop often used these words of Isaiah: "Those that wait on the Lord shall not be put to shame to all eternity."

One night after a hard day, we stood side by side in the washroom. We were exhausted and enfeebled. Both of us suffered the same ailments: fluid, lesions, dysentery, vomiting blood. We understood each other and had enjoyed several talks about fundamental spiritual questions. Van Lierop knew what sin and grace were.

That night he said to me, "I can't last much longer. I'll have to report to the infirmary soon." I was shocked, for I knew that anyone in our physical condition who took that step would be dead within a few days.

But he added, "Don't worry; I long to be with the Lord. Tomorrow, when I leave by the chimney, I want you to say the words that will also be my last words: "Those that wait on the Lord shall not be put to shame to all eternity." With brotherly love, we said goodbye to each other. We knew that it was for the last time. The next day, Arnold Van Lierop was in heaven, and I know that he will never be put to shame throughout eternity.

But for me the Lord had something other than being taken up into His eternal glory. My prayer for deliverance was not answered "through the chimney" in the form of eternal deliverance. One of my fellow prisoners, who was part of my work kommando but who was housed in one of the "free" blocks, had long been outraged at the treatment that I was receiving, so he agreed to deliver a note from me to a man in the Labor Pool called Julius, who had a reputation for fairness.

In the note I explained the intolerable situation I was in and pleaded with him to save my life for the sake of my family and my congregation. The note was delivered on Monday morning accompanied by our prayers. Tuesday at 5:30 A.M., Julius came walking over to our kommando and called out 30650—my number. To the surprise and chagrin of the subforeman, I was immediately transferred to the large kommando, Transportbaulage II. Julius talked with the foreman awhile, and then we walked off to the railroad yards.

Waiting there to be unloaded were some fifteen boxcars full of construction supplies: huge beams, boards, sewer pipes, chimneys, doors, window, bags of cement, motors, and construction steel. I was allowed to take it easy, and the foreman never once bothered me. The subforeman, instead of driving me, urged me to rest.

I did so at my own risk, however. The pace depended on the S.S. guards on duty, as some were interested only in preventing escapes; but many were fanatics who kept a sharp watch to see that the prisoners worked hard. The foreman and subforeman were convinced that I was moribund, so they paid no attention when I spent the greater part of the day lying down in an empty boxcar. When the days turned cold in November—and Dachau could get surprisingly cold—I took advantage of a huge storage area filled with crushed coal, almost as fine as dust. Such large piles of coaldust generate an amazing amount of heat below the surface; a couple of feet down it is warm enough to cook a potato. The further down you dig, the warmer it gets.

When the temperature dropped to 20 or 30 degrees below freezing, it was almost impossible to keep warm, for we had almost no outer clothing. So I constantly watched for a chance to bury myself secretly in the warmth of the coaldust to recover from the cold. At the same time, I had to be on a constant lookout for guards. Sometimes a group of us would hide in a nearby boiler room that was steaming hot.

For three weeks I was well treated in this kommando, and my physical condition stabilized. I had reached the bottom. Not that I recovered, but at least I did not continue to decline. The kommando also received extra rations of bread and lunch meats and, even though I was a clergyman, I was not excluded. But after three weeks, things changed. The subforeman of my previous kommando had discovered that, although I was in the heavy Transportbaulage, I was still alive. He had, of course, assumed that I wouldn't last long doing such heavy work.

One evil day my new kommando and my old kommando ended up working side by side unloading boxcars. It boded no good. My old subforeman and my new foreman were off to one side chatting amiably. Less than an hour later, I was confronted by a changed foreman. He began hounding me and beating me. He had discovered my crime: I was a clergyman, one of those parasites that had to be exterminated. The next day he kicked me off a railroad car, bruising several of my ribs. Then by way of apology, he knocked a few teeth out of my mouth. Although I was unable to catch my breath because of the pain, he forced me to work.

I was commanded to arrange things inside the boxcar as five other men hauled them to the door. They were bringing in all manner of materials. I had to work like a madman to keep up with five men. The foreman stood behind me with a stick and allowed me little or no hesitation in deciding where things should go. The boxcar had to be well packed so that there would be no "dead spaces"; otherwise, the cargo would shift and there would be breakage when the boxcars were banged around. In the foreman's eyes, I did nothing right and he let fly a barrage of blows every time I moved something.

This was the way of the concentration camp: a prisoner was put to work on a job that required certain skills that he did not possess. Then if he used some tool incorrectly or clumsily, or put something in the wrong place, he was not shown how to rectify his error, but he was beaten until he caught on by himself. Not all foremen operated that way, however. But most of mine did. Things had suddenly gone bad again. And they didn't get any better, for a few days later, one of the cronies of my former subforeman appeared in my kommando to help supervise my work.

Every day was a fight for survival. I couldn't possibly bear this kind of punishment for very long. I had to get out of this kommando too. In addition, unbearable hunger racked my body, and I was tortured by lack of sleep. It was unimaginable misery. And life in the blocks brought no relief.

The days from July to November were especially bad. Whenever we had a more lenient guard, we would look for a chance to tip over garbage cans as we passed through the S.S. camp or the streets of Dachau. We were thankful if we could scavenge a few potato peels or other vegetable wastes out of the dust and ashes. An apple was a real find! We also watched for crusts of bread or cheese that had been tossed out on the street for the birds. There were times when hunger pangs kept us awake most of the night.

Sending packages to Dachau was strictly forbidden, yet many relatives in Holland tried it anyway, in the hope that something might get through. In September, my wife sent me a package via the Red Cross. The commandant was kind enough to summon me for the postal inspection; I was exempted from my work kommando and had to report to the headquarters of the commandant. From 6 o'clock in the morning until 12:30, and from 1 o'clock until 7 P.M., I stood waiting outside in the hot sun—seven days in a row. At the end of each day I was called in, only to be told to come back the following day.

On the eighth day, I was called into the commandant's office. He opened the package before me, and with his murderer's hands he pawed over the delicacies that my wife had made for me. He let me have a good look at everything, and then informed me that it had all been impounded. Then, cursing eloquently, he told me to remove my carcass from his holy of holies before I came to an unholy end.

That was my first encounter with packages from home. Later, we had to report to the camp post office to receive packages; we had to pay fifty cents in postal fees, and then we saw nothing of our packages. These were tantalizing trials; hopes were raised only to be undermined and trampled. In December, however, some things began to reach us. Once I received several hard-boiled eggs, which I ate shell and all so as not to waste the precious calcium. But this amounted to just a drop of water on a hot griddle. In the barracks, things were improving slightly, but the work kommando was still calculated murder.

I don't know which was worse, the murderous summer heat and the endless days, or the ice and snow storms of winter, when we had only scanty rags to protect our starved, exhausted, festering bodies against 20 or 30 degrees of frost. Even at night we couldn't get warm, for we were packed into the blocks so tightly that the windows had to be kept open for oxygen. But our thin, worn cotton blankets could not protect us from the cold.

Sometimes we had to stand in a snowstorm for hours waiting for a train that had been delayed. When it finally did arrive, often the goods that we had to unload were covered with ice and snow. Our hands were numb and covered with frostbite sores. We lacked the strength to lift the heavy supplies. But we had to. With our clumsy wooden clogs, we had to work on top of high loads slick with ice. At the end of each day, I said a prayer of thanks that I had not fallen off. It was a miracle that I never slipped, because our foreman would not let up in the slightest, and drove us without a thought to our safety. Frequently Psalm 91 came to my mind: "For he will give his angels charge over you to guard you in all your

ways. On their hands they will bear you up, lest you dash
your foot against a stone. You will tread on the lion and the
adder; the young lion and the serpent you will trample under
foot." Neither the open attacks of the lion, nor the subtle
devices of the adder were successful in causing my downfall.

The Miracle of Answered Prayer

Meanwhile, our lives had become a matter of weeks or even days. Little by little we learned how to figure someone's life expectancy. Almost all of us clergymen in Block 28 were "goners." The great majority of us had long since passed the stage of skin-and-bones. We were getting fat again, swelling up with water—the sign of impending death. The process of starvation proceeded according to schedule in regular stages that we could observe in ourselves and in our comrades. We predicted, so-and-so had less than two days and so-and-so another week. And we thought to ourselves, "I've only got so many days, and the end of the war still isn't in sight!"

Through my letters, my wife was fully aware of the hopelessness of my situation. I mentioned nothing of the daily atrocities that I had to suffer—that would only have aggravated her suffering. But the quick succession of deaths in our camp said enough, for the wives of the Dutch clergymen in Dachau came together once a month to exchange news. At every meeting there were more widows.

Every letter out of Dachau was read to the consistories of the churches. The letter that I wrote in October was construed as a farewell letter. So the consistory in Arnhem decided to hold a prayer service for the prisoners on December 17, 1942. This could not be announced, of course. On Sunday the consistory announced that on December 17 three different meetings would be held in three different locations—one for each district of the church. They would be led by three different pastors, and the topic of discussion would be the power of prayer. The message was passed on by word of mouth that these meetings were to be prayer services for all prisoners, particularly for those in Dachau.

On December 16 I received a letter from my wife telling me of the prayer services and asking us to pray along with the congregation of Arnhem. At 8:30 the following night all the Dutch clergymen in Dachau crept together in their sleeping quarters on several mattresses and prayed. In our prayer we brought to the Lord five specific requests on which we felt our lives depended: we prayed for a new commandant, for transfer to the block for German clergymen, for fewer heavy kommandos, for more time to sleep, and for official permission to receive packages.

The next day I received three packages at one time, and nothing was confiscated from them. That same week I was transferred from the Transportbaulage Kommando to the sock-darning department. A few days before Christmas we were all moved from Block 28 to Block 26, where the German clergymen were housed and where treatment was much better. We did not have to get up as early in our new quarters either; we could sleep from 9 P.M. to 5 A.M.

In about a week, our situation had been transformed: we had gone from a death trap to a convalescent home. Behind all these astounding changes lay nothing less than a change in commandant as effected by the power of prayer. The bestial Hoffman had been sent to the Eastern Front and had been replaced by Commandant Weiss. None of us will ever forget those days. We were living in a world of miracles. After months and months of being deliberately and gradually destroyed, we were finally enjoying the wonderful privilege of getting adequate sleep and rest.

Life was immeasurably better in Block 26! A constant stream of packages arrived there; the German clergymen received packages every day. It took a while before *we* started receiving packages, however; first the news had to get back home, and then the packages from Holland took about a month to reach Dachau. Also they had to be inspected and charged import duties. The letters that we were permitted to write once a month took about three weeks to reach their destination. So it was several weeks or about mid-February before the stream of packages from the Netherlands began to arrive. But when they did, our little group of Hollanders began receiving them at least once a day, sometimes five or eight packages a day, and once, ten.

We couldn't eat all the food ourselves. But it didn't go to waste. Some prisoners weren't allowed to receive any packages whatsoever. They were mostly communists or former officers who had joined outlawed organizations. With all our packages, we were able to keep these men from starving. Every day we smuggled boxes of food to them. At times we felt guilty because of the hungry persons at home who were sending us food that they badly needed themselves.

After Christmas of 1942, we had plenty of everything. But we didn't feel free to write home and tell them to send less, because we had to think about the prisoners who never had anything. Those in the invalid blocks were forbidden to receive packages, and they were slowly dying. A few months later many of them were changed men as a result of their improved diet, and some recovered completely. We thanked God for answering our prayers, not just for ourselves, but also for the others, for the whole camp. We had so much to eat that we could almost stop eating the camp food, so we divided our ration among the other prisoners.

The Russians, for example, who never had any packages, were given double and sometimes triple rations as a result. Of the eight or ten containers of soup delivered to our block, five or six went to the Invalid or Russian Blocks. We were even able to share our rations of bread, butter, and lunch meats with our comrades. At the same time, in contrast to the good, nutritious food we got from home, the camp food began to taste more and more like the slop it was. When we were starving, we thought that the soup was delicious. We used to marvel at the fact that, although we got the same cabbage soup day after day, we never tired of it. Every day we looked forward to it. But now we gagged over cabbage and turnip soup. It reeked like a sewer.

I had arrived in my new block just a few days before Christmas and was very heartily received by my German colleagues, along with the Dutch clergymen. The men who shared a table with Idema, Hinloopen, and me seemed especially hospitable. We were in the last stages of starvation and were not yet receiving regular shipments of food packages, but they shared their supplies with us.

That Christmas was an unforgettable day. Our former commandant hadn't even given us a fifteen-minute break on Sundays or holidays. But Commandant Weiss gave us three days off for Christmas. We also had permission to stay up until midnight and to smoke in our living quarters. We had a beautiful Christmas together. Our living quarters were decorated with pine branches and a Christmas tree. Bible texts and illustrations lined the walls, and the best singers among us formed a choir to sing Christmas songs.

The German pastors had been richly supplied by their families, and in the spirit of the occasion, they had set out all their blessings—cookies, cake, rolls, fruit, and many other delicacies—on a decorated table as part of a communal love feast. Under the new commandant, roll call lasted from fifteen minutes to a half hour; therefore, our Christmas feast could begin at 7 o'clock. Christmas meditations were followed by singing, a few recitals, food and drink and light conversation.

I was reminded of the story of the pious farmer who year after year gave his wife the same birthday present: a big cake emblazoned with the words "O taste and see that the Lord is good!" It may sound a bit extreme, but in this situation, we actually seemed to be able to taste God's goodness with the taste buds on our tongues. In those first few weeks, having enough food to eat was symbolic. We ate from the abundance of God's grace. I said to my fellow pastors, we are literally tasting Psalm 103: 1-14 and 22.

That night we were caught up in a miraculous world. Yet we were in Dachau—an extermination camp where hunger, disease, and death stalked everyone, where every Christian witness was smothered in blood. Only a few weeks earlier, a Polish priest had been stomped to death because he had removed his cap when he passed the chapel. But now we were reading from God's Word, we were praying and singing, we were celebrating the birth of Christ together. And we did so, not in secret, but with the knowledge and approval of the new commandant.

On Christmas we also held our first proper worship service. And the following Sunday we held our first communion service. Kneeling around the Lord's table to receive the bread and the wine were Czech and German and Hollander. Together we shared the Lord's Supper, and together we wept. The Germans were our enemies; yet we had fellowship with the same Redeemer and Lord, Jesus Christ.

Christmas of 1942 was the turning point, in many respects. Insofar as this was possible in the concentration camp, life began to be good again, physically and spiritually. One would have to suffer a year of starvation, wearing labor, devilish treatment, and constant assault on the nervous system to know what kind of deliverance this was for us. Naturally, anyone thrown into the Dachau of 1943 from a sheltered middle-class existence would have thought it a horrible existence and would still have had plenty of reason for that judgment. But in comparison with what it had been like, Dachau had become a health resort for us. Not only were we allowed to have worship services on Sunday, but we were even allowed to hold morning devotions and vespers each day.

During the winter, we got up at 5 o'clock and had a 6

ON CHRISTMAS WE HELD OUR FIRST PROPER WORSHIP SERVICE.

o'clock roll call, so we had about half an hour to dress, wash, and have breakfast, and then half an hour for devotions. We took turns leading. We sang a few songs, read a passage from Scripture, and one of us spoke for ten minutes or so.

Vespers were held at 9 or 9:30 at night when we were all lying on our mattresses. We closed by praying the Lord's Prayer in unison, and the leader in devotions would end with "Laudatur Jesus Christus" (May Jesus Christ be Praised) and all responded, "in saecula saeculorum" (in time without end).

In just a few months, the whole face of the camp had changed. Before Christmas, we dragged our bodies to roll call and to our kommandos like skeletons, barely alive; by March, we were parading smartly through the camp streets with bounce and rhythm in our steps. Before Christmas, no laughter was heard in the camp; all joy was stifled by the grim spectre of death. A few months later, the laughter of prisoners rang out morning, noon, and night. God had worked miracles! Another commandant, more sleep, less hard labor, no senseless abuse, plenty to eat, an almost congenial life together in the barracks—*all* our requests made in mutual prayer had been answered.

Our new commandant was obviously a much different man from the preceding commander. To all S.S. guards, all foremen, and all Prominents came the order, "Respect life and respect death." And he didn't just issue orders; he visited the camp repeatedly to see that no more senseless and needless torment and torture went on. For example, one extremely cold day in January, the unemployed prisoners were standing outside in the snow, as usual, trying to keep from freezing. They were not permitted to sit or go into the barracks as long as the other prisoners were out working. Weiss, the commandant, seeing several hundred men standing around shivering, called in the camp elder and asked him what was going on: "Why are these men standing around in the cold?"

The camp elder explained that these prisoners were unassigned, and those who didn't belong to a work kommando had to stand outside from 6 o'clock in the morning until 7 at night. Weiss exploded with indignation! He sent all the prisoners back to the warmth of their barracks and threatened to take action against the prison staff if it ever happened again.

Weiss soon found out what kind of animal his predecessor had been, especially toward the clergy. They had been the most abused; they had suffered most from starvation; they had been repeatedly conscripted as laboratory animals; they had been assigned to the heaviest and dirtiest kommandos; and, understandably, they had had the highest mortality rate. Weiss must have felt obliged to make amends, for he did much for the clergymen in the camp.

It wasn't long before he was making the rounds of all the heaviest and dirtiest kommandos. The prisoners would be ordered to line up, and Weiss would call forward all the clergymen, especially those of Block 26, and ask them whether they had any complaints and whether they liked the work. Usually, they were transferred to easier, more pleasant kommandos to do something else, such as administrative work.

He also made several fundamental changes in camp leadership, insofar as it was in the hands of the prisoners. The key positions, as I have pointed out, were filled by communists: the infirmary, the "nice" kommandos with easy work and a chance to organize some food, the Labor Pool, etc. And those leaders had passed the best jobs on to other communists. They had made it virtually impossible for a clergyman to get on a work kommando in which a person could survive, or on one that received extra bread rations. Leadership positions at work, in the blocks, or in the rooms were also closed to the clergy.

Clergymen were also invariably assigned to the worst beds in the infirmary when they became sick. Typically, however, a clergyman who reported sick was kicked away from the infirmary door and sent back to work. Even if he were running a high temperature and seemed close to death, he was chased off as a shirker. To be hospitalized, however, was even more dangerous. The great majority of clergymen admitted in the evening were dead the next morning. If they weren't, they were used as laboratory animals. Only those who had a communist friend to speak for them were admitted for helpful treatment.

Apparently Weiss found out about these internal abuses. He promptly rid the infirmary of the worst violators and made theirs and other openings available to clergymen, who were asked to volunteer for the jobs. In mid-January, an epidemic of typhoid fever broke out, so Weiss called for men who would genuinely care for the sick, and who were willing to risk their own lives against the disease. He had many volunteers from the clergy. In this way, the infirmary had a sudden influx of orderlies who took the work not in order to steal the bread of the sick, but actually to nurse them back to health.

One who has been almost starved to death can eat huge amounts the first few weeks without having his hunger satisfied, without ever feeling full. Several prisoners actually died from the food packages. They couldn't discipline themselves to increase their intake gradually. All their organs had been weakened and had shrunk. Their digestive systems could not possibly work at full capacity. Some made too great a demand on their organs by suddenly eating large amounts of rich foods.

It was a blessing that December was a kind of transition time, during which more and more food gradually became available as packages began arriving slowly. The cigars that came in my first packages were used to organize bread and soup from the kitchen workers, who could eat all they wanted. One small cigar brought me ten potatoes or a little pan of soup; a large cigar, half a loaf of bread or sometimes even a whole loaf. The big influx of food didn't start until mid-January, however.

At the same time, a plague of lice caused a typhoid epidemic, especially among the Russians, so that almost all work kommandos were confined to their barracks. For six weeks they did no work; our sleeping hours were increased in order to build up our strength and resistance; and strict hygiene was enforced in the bathrooms. We took turns supervising the bathrooms to see that no one left without scrubbing both himself and the toilet.

We had a short roll call at 7 in the morning and another short one at 7 in the evening. There was inside work each day, and every day there were packages arriving in our block; hence, it became possible for us to eat all day long. The variety of foods we received from occupied countries was unbelievable: butter, fat, oil, cheese, bacon, fruits, bread, cake, sweets, syrup, cans of milk, sugar, canned meat, sausages, sardines, salmon, cocoa, and all kinds of vegetables. Several companies (directly or through our wives) sent us foods containing iron, calcium, protein, and vitamin supplements to build up our bodies again.

Once, all the Dutch clergy got a shipment of one hundred bottles of currant juice from a company in The Hague, and on other occasions we all were sent jam, applesauce, and canned fruit. From another company we received boxes of grapes and delicious eating apples. We were finally being well taken care of, and we praised God every day!

For six weeks we did nothing but eat. We ate prodigious amounts! We ate so much that we couldn't believe our own eyes. It was incredible! Idema, Hinloopen and I formed a common "pot" to share all our food. We made a little commune. During those first six weeks, every day each of us ate 4 liters (7 pints) of soup, thirty potatoes smothered in bacon and butter, 1 can of vegetables, 1 can of liver paste, 1 can of sardines, 1 can of salmon, 1/2-pound of cheese, 1 cheese, 1 can of sausages, half a jar (sometimes a whole jar) of jam, 2 oz. of butter, almost 2 pounds of bread, 1 pound of cake, cookies, and biscuits, and fruit.

Also, three times a day we took a series of 5 to 10 diet supplements (cod liver oil, calcium, iron, protein, and vitamins from A to Z with a multivitamin to top it off). We did not take these supplements in the usual dosages because the label read "Except by prescription." We prescribed *multiple* doses for ourselves, and we ate all day long. Only after about six weeks of this did our hunger begin to abate.

Hunger, it seems, has little to do with the amount of food contained in your digestive tract, but depends on how much nutrition and strength the body has stored up. Our bodies had been deprived so long and needed so much that we could keep stuffing ourselves for several weeks without becoming satisfied. For six weeks, never once did our bodies cry, "Enough!" but kept saying, "More! More!" Sometimes we thought that our stomachs could never again be filled.

We said of one another, "Where does he put it all?" Some ate so much that I won't challenge your credulity by listing it all. Even I find it hard to believe—and I saw it! Finally, after about six weeks of this, came the historic moment when one after another we began to say, "I'm not hungry anymore!" After that, we ate very little for a few weeks, and then we returned to normal eating habits. We ate well, but we ate sensibly.

I tremble to say it, but we became the capitalists of the camp. Our packages made us powerful. This placed a serious responsibility on us, namely, to use our riches justly and mercifully in the camp—responsibly toward both God and man. Each of us had friends in our work kommandos who were not getting packages, and we shared our riches with them. We also felt responsible for our fellow countrymen in the Invalid Block and elsewhere. Every day we collected food for those in the infirmary, for those with stomach problems and dysentery—who needed special diets, and for those sick with typhoid—who needed fruit. So our wealth was not just a blessing to those of us who got packages, but also to those who didn't. Not only did everyone share in our wealth, they also got double rations from the camp kitchen because we had almost stopped eating camp food.

Meanwhile, we gradually grew bolder in the camp as our freedom increased. In our living quarters we had a large square stove. It was a very efficient model that produced much heat and stayed warm long after the fire had died. To cook or heat anything on the stove, however, was strictly forbidden. Furthermore, we had to keep our little pans shining like a mirror. Once put on the stove, they would have been permanently discolored. So we organized tin cans and S.S. mess kits to cook our food. But that didn't solve the problem; there wasn't enough room on the stove for everyone to get their cooking done during our breaks. Every one of us had something to warm up, cook, bake, or fry. But we found a solution! We contacted the prisoners who worked in a factory that assembled electrical parts. They smuggled out parts and put together makeshift hotplates for us. To own one of these, singly or with a group, was the pinnacle of affluence.

A great transformation had been brought about in our camp life. God had greatly limited the powers of hell. We had a hard time comprehending the extent of His blessing. Again and again, we compared our lives with what they had been only a few weeks before. It was a miracle of His mercy! We saw it, and eagerly, thankfully, accepted it but we didn't understand it.

The Chess Game with the S.S.

As our circumstances improved, we entered into a chess game with the S.S. Every time the S.S. made a move to make life more difficult for us, we made a countermove to neutralize it.

It was quite a game. But not everyone wanted to play. Many prisoners went about their tasks obediently, and dutifully followed the orders issued by the S.S. Survival was their only aim. The work was no longer as heavy as before, nor the tempo as inhuman; and the food was more than enough. So they left well enough alone. But some of us, especially the Dutch, had something else in mind—sabotage! Our goal was to do nothing whatsoever to help the Nazi cause. And soon we were doing virtually nothing in the camp. If all human goals were realized as well as we realized our goal in Dachau, the world would be a much better place.

Through the influence we achieved with our packages and the protection of Weiss, we clergymen could pick almost any work kommando we wished. Not without a certain amount of daring and risk, of course, for many of the Prominents were still hostile to us. But we eventually managed to get our way.

The only three clergymen in the Sock-darning Kommando were my two colleagues Janus and Hinloopen and I. We spent the entire day in a dark, dank cellar, patching socks and mittens. I could write a book just on our adventures in this kommando. It was from here that we played our chess game against the S.S. We were supposed to work eleven hours a day in our kommando, but we managed to put in less than two hours a day. Some days we didn't show up at all.

But we had a good time together. We had no wish to leave our filthy cellar and the filthy socks and the even filthier rags used to patch them. Small holes—those that were the size of your heel or all your toes—were darned. Large holes—those that took up over half the sock—were patched with rags made from old camp uniforms and from the clothes of deceased prisoners. We also made mittens for the prisoners. We cut them out according to a cardboard pattern and sewed the two parts together by hand. The trickiest part was making the thumb look decent. Even if I say so myself, Hinloopen and I became very adept at this job. Soon it will become clear why we loved our filthy cellar and why we wouldn't have traded our dirty kommando for any other.

Once I nearly became a victim of Commandant Weiss's generosity. One morning we all had to be on the job because Weiss was scheduled to inspect our cellar. We worked like model prisoners. When Weiss and his staff came bursting in, all the clergymen from Block 26 were asked to muster outside. There we waited at attention. When Weiss and his entourage came outside, he was still carrying on about "that damned pigsty," "that hell hole," and other similar expletives.

There was some truth to his remarks. The cellar *was* a stinking mess. Yet it also had a certain attractiveness, a quaint atmosphere like an old shoemaker's shop. Weiss asked a couple of clergymen what they thought of working "in that sewer." Before anyone could respond, he answered himself: it was a rotten shame that intellectuals like us had to live in such filth. He had a more pleasant kommando for us, one

I COULD WRITE A BOOK JUST ON OUR ADVENTURES IN
THE SOCK-DARNING KOMMANDO.

more appropriate to our calling—the payroll department. He meant well, but to me it was a dark day. There was no way out, however; for we were immediately marched over to the Labor Pool to be transferred to the ministry of finance of the S.S.

I tried to get my name taken off the list later that morning, but no one would do it. Everyone looked at me as if I were crazy! Who would rather work in a dark, stinking basement than in a clean ground-floor office? I was asked, what on earth possessed me. But I couldn't very well tell anyone why I preferred to stay in the cellar and how I spent my time there. So I just replied, "Everyone to his own taste." But now the problem was, how could I get out of the new kommando; could I somehow refuse the privilege that had been forced upon me?

My friend Hinloopen was spared this difficulty, for he was in the infirmary that day with swollen legs. We had been eating well for several months and had recovered most of our strength. Our lesions had also healed. But fluid was still a problem. Our legs took at least half a year to get back to normal. Even two years after our imprisonment, our legs would still swell up after a hard day.

The next day we marched off with our elite kommando to the large building in the S.S. camp that housed the payroll department. Idema was with us too; he had been liberated from another kommando. As novices we first had to do the work of office boys. Then we were to be promoted to typing, answering correspondence, keeping statistics, or maintaining the files. To start with, six of us were put in a room to recycle old envelopes by pasting over the old addresses.

The S.S. officer who supervised us was an amiable fellow who did his best to impress the "gentlemen." He was extremely polite and granted us considerable freedom, leaving us unsupervised most of the day. Now and then he would come in and talk for a half hour or so. Our German colleagues, who had a slightly different perspective from that of us foreigners, worked steadily to a constant stream of banter and light conversation. We concluded that since they got so much done, we were excused from doing anything.

Once a day or so the Obersturmfuehrer, the head of the whole department, came storming in to see whether everyone were working. He was a highly temperamental man, exceedingly impressed with his own importance and power. He let it be known that we ought to consider it a great privilege to work here and that, therefore, he demanded total effort from us. Otherwise, we were not wanted and would be returned to the filthy, backbreaking work of our old kommando; that is we would be kicked out of the payroll department for "Lumpheit, Brutalitaet, Frechheit, und Faulheit" (cruelty, rudeness, insolence, and laziness).

So the next day we smuggled a pipe, some tobacco, and a newspaper into the office. When we got there, we didn't go to work at all, but we made ourselves comfortable, putting our feet up on another chair, lighting up a pipe and brazenly reading the paper. We hoped, albeit with fear and trembling, that the Obersturmfuehrer would come in and, catching us loafing, kick us out of his elite kommando back to our dirty cellar. But we were afraid that in his outrage, he might do worse. We might also be sentenced to twenty-five lashes. But nothing ventured, nothing gained. Without taking risks, we couldn't very well expect to carry out our goals in the concentration camp.

We smoked, loafed, and chatted all morning, but the Obersturmfuehrer, whose arrival we both desired and dreaded, did not come. We told each other that even if he *never* showed up, we would have an easy life of it, and we would not be helping the S.S.

After dinner, we picked up more reading matter and settled down as before. Halfway through the afternoon, the door burst open and the big moment arrived. Never had I seen anyone look so dumbfounded, and never have I seen anyone become so furious! Instead of leaping to attention, we tapped our pipes, shuffled our newspapers, and, slowly disentangling our legs from the chairs, we lurched to our feet. He called us every name in the book and then announced that we would all be subjected to a humiliating punishment. We were all fired from the privileged positions and left to fend for ourselves.

That evening at roll call we got another raking over from our foreman, and we were told that we had been dropped from the elite kommando. Our plan had worked beautifully. We had won this move in our chess game against the S.S. The next morning I went strolling back triumphantly to my old cellar, and I was greeted with a big cheer. My co-workers knew that I esteemed my "despised friends" in my "despised cellar" far more than the cultured gentlemen in the Ministry of Finance.

Why was I so attached to my cellar? It had become a symbol of resistance and daring to me and my colleagues. Something was always going on. Here I had found a calling. Besides, the place was alive with humor. The composition of this kommando of 190 men was unique. You had only to see us. We made quite a spectacle marching from the parade ground to the cellar—a parade of rejects. We were a deformed and twisted company. Our kommando was not for the young and healthy who were fit for manual labor. It was a kommando for the elderly, the lame, the crippled, the amputees, the deaf, and for a few younger men who had friends in the Labor Pool.

The foreman of this motley company was named Wilhelm. He alone is worth a psychological study; he alone could supply enough material for a comic novel about the underground men of Dachau. He was unbelievably naive and at the same time as sly as a fox. He was a primitive with a strong instinct for survival. Abstractions and concepts were beyond him; he couldn't think or speak in terms of general truths or ideas. He expressed himself in terms of stories and life drama. He was not a book of words, but a picture book, sometimes without any words at all.

At times the kommando became careless and got far too noisy during working hours, risking severe punishment should an S.S. man suddenly drop in. In order to warn his men, Wilhelm would not say, "Quiet down, men! Take it easy, or we'll all be punished!" Instead, he would act out the whole situation. First, he would shout "Ruhe!" (Silence). Immediately there would be absolute silence, for we knew that we were in for a show. Wilhelm would find a spot in the middle of the cellar, and he would begin by doing a humorous imitation of some of the loudest and gabbiest prisoners. Then he would parody the thundering fury of an S.S. man exploding into the room and catching the goof-offs in the act. Finally, we would see enacted the dismay and mortification of the prisoners who had been foolish enough to be caught napping. He was able to invent endless variations on this same theme, so that we never got the same show twice.

Wilhelm was one of the best foremen in the camp. He had never beaten another prisoner, and he took pride in the fact. He tried to create camaradarie and solidarity among the prisoners. His heart went out to them. If his kommando managed to organize something extra, he would be as happy as a little child. He had connections in the kitchen, and, occasionally, an extra container of soup or pail of potatoes would find its way into the cellar. When the food packages began to pour into camp, he saw to it that no one in the kommando was starving.

Although he was a good man, Wilhelm knew exactly what his limits were. He would take many risks, but he had an excellent nose for approaching danger. It seemed almost as if he had developed an extra sense. He loved to needle the intellectuals, but he was proud that he had many friends among them. He was obviously delighted when one of us dropped in on him during our free time and invited him for a walk along the camp streets or for a bull session in our block. We often shared treats from our packages with him. Soon we developed an easy-going, friendly relationship with each other. From the beginning we exploited our favorable situation to the fullest.

Under the Nazi system of injustice, we did only what we

were absolutely forced to do. Most humiliating were the in-justices that were upheld by brute force. To be compelled to submit to a group of degenerates and criminals was almost in-tolerable. Moreover, we had been imprisoned without the slightest legal grounds, so we felt free to sabotage wherever we could. Every chance we got, we ducked out of work. Hinloopen and I agreed on this strategy. We began to get a reputation for being saboteurs and freebooters, sometimes to the great chagrin of those servile souls with a misplaced sense of responsibility and an unhealthy conscience.

Constantly courting severe punishment, and taking tremendous risks, for six months we subverted all order and regulations. Again and again, stricter measures were passed to detect, oppose, and punish our misdeeds. But every time we in turn took counter-measures. Refusal to work was con-sidered one of the greatest crimes that a prisoner could com-mit. It was sabotage! So a rigorous system of checks had been set up. During working hours—from six in the morning until seven at night, except for one hour at noon— we were supposed to be working constantly.

But being absent from one's kommando was an even greater crime than inactivity. It was not only very difficult to absent oneself without being caught, it was also very dangerous. In fact, if we were in a kommando that worked outside the camp proper, it was impossible. Every komman-do was counted and registered when it left and again when it returned so that everyone could be accounted for. Arbitrary spot checks were held during the day to keep tabs on the kommandos.

To leave such a kommando was to risk your life, for if you were missing during one of the spot checks, you were con-sidered to be an escapee and were punished accordingly. You couldn't even leave work to go to the latrine without a pass from your foreman. Anyone caught away from his komman-do without such a pass was severely punished. The latrines were checked regularly for malingerers who lacked passes.

It was strictly forbidden to us to be on the camp streets

during working hours or to go back to our block. The camp police patrolled the grounds all day, checking the passes of the prisoners who occasionally appeared on the street. A pass was supposed to indicate that we were on a specific errand. It consisted of a block of wood stamped with a red seal. Part of the job of the block and room elders, who were the only ones authorized to be in the barracks during working hours, was to see that nobody else stayed behind. In addition, S.S. soldiers, and numerous squad and block leaders were continually passing through the camp. Every day we had to devise new ways to beat the system. But this was a great game, and we became increasingly imaginative. The first few months were very difficult. But we did not give up! We persisted until our illegal practices began to be recognized as rights—rights which once won would not easily be relinquished.

One way we outwitted our keepers was by acquiring one of the camp's wooden passes for our personal use. With it we could walk about the camp any time of the day. The tricky part was entering our own block, for if anyone saw us, we were lost. It was imperative that we slip through one of the windows of our sleeping quarters and reached one of the top bunks unseen. Then we could catch a few hours sleep. But we had to get back to our kommando before the end of our working hours, that is, at 11:30 in the morning and at 7 o'clock in the evening, so that we would be present when our kommando marched past the checkpoint. Otherwise, we would be recorded as missing.

When Wilhelm, our foreman, finally caught on to our trick, he gave us a dressing down in his own entertaining manner and took away our pass. Then he told us to follow him to the Labor Pool to be reported. So we followed Wilhelm outside. Less than ten steps outside our cellar door, we had pacified Wilhelm and averted the danger. It cost us a Ritmeester cigar and a hunk of cheese.

It also gave us a chance to discuss our plans and our problems with him. He sympathized with our ideals, but there were limits to his permissiveness. He could also get into trouble, he reminded us, especially if he were betrayed by someone in the kommando, which was an ever-present possibility. So we in turn sympathized with him in his difficult situation. And we assured him that if we were ever caught, we would take full responsibility for our actions.

A half hour or so later we re-entered the cellar and put on the most guilt-stricken pose that we could muster. Wilhelm treated us with cold anger, as though we had been given only twenty-four hours to live. A solemn, impressive silence hung over the kommando. We played our roles to the hilt, and we loved every minute of it.

Hinloopen and I and several Polish clergymen had the honor of comprising a special kommando to assist in the clothing rooms on the floors above. This kommando was needed for varying amounts of time during the last few hours of the working day. This task presented us with new opportunities for sabotage. We would sign out with our foreman to go to work upstairs, and after messing about in the clothing department awhile, we would sign out with the foreman there. The latter thought that we were going to work downstairs. In actuality, we would pick our way through the camp police, and soon we would be snoozing peacefully in our barracks.

But one day we found out how great was the risk that we were taking. While we were sleeping like innocent children, the foreman of the clothing room went downstairs to Wilhelm to fetch the two Dutch preachers to work for him. They traded words, each asserting, "I signed them out to you!" The upstairs foreman was livid and immediately sounded the alarm to the camp police. The message went out that two prisoners from Block 26 were either attempting escape or had left their kommando and were guilty of sabotage. We were rudely awakened by the shouts of the camp police.

They were looking for us! We had to stay out of the hands of the camp police at all costs; otherwise, we would be turned in for punishment. Our lives were in danger! But we had planned for just such an occasion and had made preparations.

Above the ceiling in our sleeping quarters was a small crawl space. We had cut out a part of the ceiling not visible from the floor because of the high bunks and made a little trap door. It was our secret hiding place, not just for ourselves but also for some of our food.

To have more than one food package in your possession was illegal. But sometimes we would get ten packages in a single day. In such instances, we always, of course, divided the food among the prisoners. But we thought it wise to keep back a small cache. After all, we were in a concentration camp; our permission to receive packages might be revoked at any time. And what if the English should land and cut Germany off from Holland? Starvation, exhaustion, disease, and death would be back in short order. A hiding place made good sense to us.

After hearing the shouts and orders, it took us only a matter of seconds to get into our asylum. We waited until the police had left. Our next move was to try to get back to our cellar kommando as quickly as possible—and without being seen. Soon we were back in our proper places among our comrades. In his own inimitable style, Wilhelm flew off the handle at us and demanded even stiffer punishments than the camp police. They ought to turn us over to him! He would make short work of us. It was a performance calculated to take the pressure off us. When it came right down to it, he *never* betrayed his men. In the end, the matter was left in Wilhelm's hands. And that's as far as it went.

By August, our living quarters were beginning to look quite cozy. Under the former commandant, we had been allowed in this room only in our bare feet, and then for only a few minutes as, in frenzied haste, we bolted down a little watery soup while standing up. Now, on one side of the room someone was cooking oatmeal on an organized hot plate, and someone else was preparing brown beans. From the other side of the room came the sizzle of baking potatoes and the smell of frying trout that had been obtained from the S.S. In one corner of the room, a group of men were enjoying a four-

or five-course dinner, as if they were in an elegant restaurant. Suddenly, someone shouted, "Achtung!" (Attention). A few seconds later an angry S.S. man appeared in the doorway.

But in a flash the room had been transformed. Nobody was eating and nobody was cooking or frying. Several men were busy scrubbing their lockers; the rest of the men had disappeared. The windows stood wide open so that a strong cross draft had already carried the many cooking odors outdoors. The S.S. man marched into the room. One of the prisoners shouted "Achtung!" and everyone leaped to attention. We reported the number of men housed in our room and explained that the prisoners present were not at work because they all had hearings of some kind or other.

After hollering and fuming about a few trivialities, the S.S. man left, satisfied that everything was in order. In a few minutes, everyone was doing what he had been before the alarm, preparing or serving or eating his food. We always saw to it that we had a prior warning before the word "Achtung" rang out, except when one of the "grandpas" was on patrol. Then we just continued with whatever we were doing. Those old fellows would just stand around making small talk and licking their chops in the hope that they would get a few leftovers. By 1943, we were eating much better than the S.S. guards.

Every hour of the day, then, we were in this exciting chess game against the S.S., with moves and counter-moves. By undermining discipline and through dogged persistence we had won certain privileges that we never again wanted to give up. Again and again, our newly won lifestyle was threatened, as the camp leaders legislated stiffer and stiffer penalties for anyone's being in the barracks during working hours. The patrols were increased and the camp police reinforced. Foremen, block and room elders were held responsible to see to it that their men remained with their work kommandos all day.

But nothing seemed to help. Again and again, we found breaks in the S.S. net that allowed us to slip through.

Hinloopen and I took great pleasure in sitting in our barracks doing whatever we wished less than a half hour after the latest S.S. threats had been announced. We hated the S.S. regulations!

We finally came to the conclusion that both of us had criminal natures by birth, for we excelled at dreaming up new ways to get around the law. We agreed that when we returned home, we would have to turn ourselves in for rehabilitation so that we could be made into decent, law-abiding citizens once again. It goes without saying, however, that we regarded our disobedience as a holy disobedience, because we were unwilling to obey demonic orders that had no right or claim to authority over us whatsoever.

Our lives were full of humor, but underneath that humor lay the strength of faith that continually recognized God as the One who answers prayer. This God made it possible for us to live as thankfully as we did, despite our being under the rule of murderers like Himmler. Himmler did not have the final word over our lives, however. God did—and only God!

Celebration in Dachau

How could anybody be in the mood for celebrating in a concentration camp, especially in Dachau? Between 1933 and Christmas of 1942, it would have been unthinkable in Dachau. During that time, Dachau saw nothing that even faintly resembled celebration of God's comfort and nearness by those tormented souls who lived, suffered, and died in Christ. Normal human happiness had been completely out of the question. There was simply nothing in the camp to be cheerful about.

But after the miraculous answer to prayer, God also provided for an earthlier joy. The new commandant encouraged the prisoners to organize all kinds of activities: sports, entertainment, and even the arts. Once the men had recovered from the fatigue of starvation, soccer matches were set up almost every day. Nationality competed against nationality, block against block, and kommando against kommando. Every so often, a big ring was constructed on the parade ground so that the whole camp could see boxing or wrestling matches.

The murderous discipline of the former commandant, it was becoming clear, had ceased for good. All attempts to deprive us of the new freedom that we had won under the milder regimen of the new commandant were futile. Everything indicated that the great power of the Third Reich was eroding. A remarkable spirit possessed all the prisoners—they no longer took their situation seriously. Everyone sensed that the end was coming, that Germany's defeat was inevitable. Many guards too, began to see the madness of the Dachau machine; and he who no longer believes in something, finds it hard to devote himself to it. Of course, the prisoners, given an inch of freedom, soon took at least a yard. The German clergymen, for example, staged a play in our room poking fun not only of each other but also of Hitler, Goering, Goebbels, Himmler, and other "benefactors" of mankind. That evening there wasn't an S.S. uniform to be seen anywhere in the vicinity.

The situation had changed so drastically that now we went out looking for other work kommandos on our own initiative. The most sought-after jobs were on the Post Office and Parcel Kommando. It was an ideal kommando because it was a night shift. You worked from 3:30 A.M. until 9:30 A.M. and then you were legally free the rest of the day. You could go wherever you wished, and you were even allowed to take an afternoon nap in the barracks.

My colleague Van Raalte was already on this kommando; he worked at the camp post office. Commandant Weiss had specified that he wanted clergymen exclusively on this kommando in order to prevent embezzlement and stealing from the parcels. This was a smart move on his part, not just because it was flattering to us clergymen to be counted among the most trustworthy in the camp. But from a purely pragmatic viewpoint it was a smart move, for the clergymen received more packages than anyone else, because they had more outside contacts than anyone else. They, therefore were rarely tempted to steal food. What could they do with it when most of them got ten times as much as they could eat?

In August, Hinloopen and I managed to wangle our way into Van Raalte's kommando. Our job was not at the post office, however, but outside the camp. At 3:30 in the morning we were already sitting in the postal truck at the railroad station in Dachau along with five other men and two guards. We no longer had to pull the heavy trucks ourselves; now we rode in them. The guards no longer beat and drove us as we worked; rather, they treated us very politely. Where we had formerly heard, "Hustle! Hustle! Let's go, you miserable filth! You good-for-nothings!" we now heard, "Please, gentlemen."

The first part of our new job was to get the carts of parcels from the station and bring them to the trucks. In the trucks, we sorted the parcels. Some had to be sent on, others went to Munich to be charged import duties, and the rest were put in carts that we later wheeled to the post office. The latter was located directly across the street from the railroad station.

By this time it was 6:30 A.M., and time for a leisurely breakfast—our second of the day. The S.S. guards ate with us. What a difference! They had a dry piece of army bread, while we had delicious sandwiches made with homemade bread from our parcels. Usually, we also had cake and cookies and several kinds of fruit. A strange world indeed! But all in the hands of God! Gradually we had traded places: now we had become gentlemen, and the S.S. guards had become the wretches, eating dry bread and facing a bleak future. They knew it too. Several of the S.S. squad leaders, who took turns accompanying us on our job, told us as much openly and made no attempt to conceal their fear of the future.

After we had eaten, we went to the post office to do more sorting. Some parcels and letters had to stay in the town of Dachau, some were meant for the S.S., and some were for the prison camp. Every day we picked up from one-to two-thousand packages for the prisoners. To have a part in this was very satisfying. It still seemed like a miracle! Sometimes it was impossible to believe the dramatic changes taking place. Instead of systematic starvation and extermination, in many respects we were now better off than those outside, and we were certainly much better off than our guards.

After loading the trucks, we rode back to the camp. A few dozen parcels were dropped off at the S.S. post office, but by far the greater part went to the prisoners' post office. After we unloaded them, another crew on our kommando sorted the parcels according to the various blocks and then delivered them. Our job was finished. We received our extra bread ration and some cold meats; this food was soon passed on to friends in the mills who needed a little extra to eat.

By now it was about 9:30 A.M. We went to wash up and had our third breakfast and a cup of cocoa. Then I lit up a cigar and sat down to read or study for a couple of hours until it was time to prepare dinner. We had virtually stopped eating the camp cabbage soup. We preferred baked potatoes, canned vegetables, cucumbers and tomatoes, with oatmeal for dessert.

Although cooking and baking were officially forbidden, we managed to get away with it day after day. It took considerable organizing. However, we had to obtain wood, coal, and peat for the big stove and also electric hot plates. Our kommando offered plenty of opportunity. Early next morning, before very many yard workers or policemen had arrived, we worked in the rail yards close to row after row of boxcars loaded with goods. Here we could organize almost anything we needed.

One day we would bring a basketful of coal; the next, a sackful of potatoes, or wood, or carrots, or onions. We would simply hide them underneath the piles of parcels. It was a risky business, and once in a while we found ourselves in some rather tense situations. But, in this way we were at least getting back a little of what had been plundered from our homelands. Thus, our kommando was unusually rewarding in every respect. Now that we were fed, the six hours of exercise that the mail-sorting gave us was very healthful. And the major part of the day was left for study, reading, discussion, preparing meals, and ministering to the other prisoners. The morale of the camp seemed to improve day by day, especially after we gained access to radio broadcasts a couple times a day and we could all follow the course of the war.

The day that Italy surrendered was an especially remarkable day. Our kommando heard the news early in the morning. It was a bright, sunny day. The drab concentration camp that otherwise looked so somber and foreboding appeared almost festive. There was a feeling in the air as if the day had been declared a national holiday. Most of the Dutch prisoners were soon walking around with marigolds in their lapels—orange being the color of the Dutch royal family, known as the House of Orange.

The S.S. officers were jumpy and irritable. That night on the parade ground, Lagerfuehrer Redwitz paced in front of the long rows of prisoners, ranting at us and letting us know, unmistakably, that, even *if* Germany lost the war, we had better not count on getting out of the camp alive. He was determined to squelch our jubilation. The festive mood among the prisoners was unnerving the Germans.

The most memorable day for the Dutch colony in camp was the celebration of Queen Wilhelmina's birthday on August 31, 1943. Although at the time it was impossible to celebrate this national holiday anywhere in the Netherlands, we celebrated it right in the lion's den, under the very nose of Himmler. Several days before the event, the Dutch colony in Dachau laid its plans. We reasoned that the S.S. would probably be unaware that August 31 was the birthday of our queen and that orange was the color of our royal family. This gave us the temerity to begin organizing a big celebration in our block.

First, we ordered big bunches of marigolds from the prisoners working on the farm kommando. A few pieces of bacon, butter, and cheese paid for an incredible number of marigolds. We decorated the whole room with them and put glasses with marigolds on all the tables. Everywhere we looked, we saw the color orange. We even wore orange on our zebra suits. Moreover, all the Dutch clergymen resolved

AUGUST 31, 1943 — THE QUEEN'S BIRTHDAY.

to take a day off on August 31 (only about twenty of us were left). We all invented an excuse. Some reported sick; others had supposedly been excused by the paymaster or by the doctor or dentist. Most of us never reported at all. We just didn't show up.

On the morning of the big day we were all busy preparing an elaborate dinner for the afternoon. Everyone had been assigned a specific task. In the last few months, we had discovered who had what gifts when it came to cooking. The menu was a huge success! That afternoon the following dishes were set among the marigolds:

Various Appetizers
Queen Wilhelmina Soup
Macaroni with Grated Cheese and Ham
Beef, Baked Potatoes and Green Beans
Chicken and Applesauce
Pudding with Currant Sauce
Fruit
Bonbons and a Pre-war Cigar

Through prisoners who worked in the factories of Munich, we also managed to organize some real Munich beer to use as a table wine.

At the climax of the afternoon's festivities, our oldest colleague delivered a fervid oration in honor of the House of Orange and Queen Wilhelmina. At that moment our German comrades came in from work. They stood respectfully at attention while we concluded the toast and ended by singing a few lines from the "Wilhelmus," the national anthem. Then we drank to the return of the queen and her government and to the fall of Hitler's Third Reich.

When the celebration was over and we were marching to the 7 o'clock roll call, we told each other, "We'd better keep this hush-hush, or else we'll end up in a concentration camp."

But a concentration camp is a place of extreme contradictions. One man gets away with stealing a cow while another gets punished for looking over the fence; one group gets away with staging a full-scale festivity, while another gets caught and punished for some petty violation. This became especially evident on that memorable August 31 of 1943. We had enjoyed a beautiful day together. It had been more like a reunion or conference than a prison camp. We had almost forgotten that we were a bunch of condemned outcasts. As we marched to the parade square, still in a festive mood, we didn't know what a dismal ending our bright day would have. But when we arrived at the square, we saw, in the center, the dreaded vaulting horse, on which prisoners who had been reported took their punishment—twenty-five lashes with a rod.

What crimes had been committed? One prisoner had been caught loafing during working hours; another was caught taking a few illicit drags on a cigarette butt; and yet another was suspected of making an escape attempt. After roll call, Lagerfuehrer Redwitz read the crimes of the twenty prisoners who had been reported. For a couple of hours it seemed as if we had been transported back to the bloody regimen of 1942. Had it been up to Redwitz and the other Lagerfuehrer, the conditions of 1942 would have been restored immediately. But Weiss was their superior and would have none of it.

Many things flashed through our minds. We thought, if Redwitz and his aids knew what was going on: that we had done hardly any work for over half a year; that we had sabotaged everything that wasn't in the prisoner's interests; that we were continually smoking, not just cigarette butts but whole cigars during working hours; and that we didn't organize just an occasional potato or onion, but whole sackfuls of them and of many other things, then twenty vaulting horses, or for that matter, twenty nooses wouldn't have been enough to satisfy their rage! Suppose Redwitz found out about our Queen's Day celebration! The illusion that we were merely out camping in Dachau had been shattered. A concentration camp was still a concentration camp. Anything could happen at any time.

When the victims came forward and lined up to wait their turn like sheep being brought to the slaughter, we said to ourselves, "Never forget this moment! One day the people who commit these atrocities will be punished!" On one side of the vaulting horse stood the sentenced men, and on the other, the block elders, nearly thirty of them. In front stood Redwitz and his staff. We noticed that a few of the old S.S. squad leaders had secretly drifted away. They had no wish to look on, much less run the chance of being selected to do the flogging. But as prisoners we had no choice but to witness this product of twentieth-century German culture.

This was a chance for Redwitz to demonstrate his authority, and he would not have us miss it. The block elders, prisoners themselves, were ordered to tie the first victim onto the horses, and then, two at a time, they were told to administer the punishment. One block elder, a tall, upright man stood in front, deathly pale, trembling with tension and revulsion. He and another elder had been ordered to work over the second man. Redwitz gave the order to lay on. Our block elder shook his head emphatically. He refused. He had sabotaged the whipping! What would happen next, we asked each other. In 1942 it would have meant certain death.

Redwitz was beside himself with incredulous fury. He threatened every kind of punishment that occurred to him. It had been the most flagrant demonstration of sabotage that the camp had ever seen, but our block elder and his colleague continued to shake their heads in refusal. The entire camp held its breath in suspense. What would be the outcome?

Redwitz made another try. He promised to give each man twenty-five lashes himself if they didn't obey. But even this threat did not work, and, therefore, even more block elders appeared to take courage, for more of them adamantly refused to carry out the order. Those who did obey, hit the offenders with such restraint that the pain was tolerable.

Only one block elder, a man from the Russian block, laid on the whip with a will. We will remember him, we assured each other. Meanwhile, Redwitz was becoming apoplectic.

He had seen it! The discipline and the fear of the S.S. had evaporated. He and the other officers could no longer ask whatever they pleased and see it done. A year earlier, such resistance would have been unthinkable. Then, every whim of the S.S. was law. But no longer!

After the first ten prisoners had received a half-hearted flogging, Redwitz could not control himself any longer. He and his men took the rods from the block elders and began flogging in earnest. The poor wretches still awaiting their turn would have to bear the full brunt of the S.S. frenzy. The moans and screams of the prisoners cut into the whole camp. Their bleeding bodies had to be carried off to the infirmary afterward.

So ended our beautiful holiday. As we marched back to our barracks, we shuddered at our brazenness. If Redwitz ever discovered our mode of living or our Queen's Day celebration, we were as good as dead.

Nevertheless, we continued to flout the S.S. orders and prohibitions whenever possible. It was not just a game; it was the only way we could nurture our spirit of resistance and keep it alive.

Freedom

Then came that momentous day of October 8, 1943. I had been taken prisoner exactly twenty months before. The foreman of the Post Office Kommando wanted to go along that morning to check things out, so I was given the morning off, and I didn't have to get up before 3:30 A.M. as I did normally. I could have slept until 5 o'clock, but I didn't; I got up at 4 o'clock. Why, I don't know.

That morning I just couldn't stay in bed. Yet it was no problem at all for me on other days. I had just washed myself and was in the process of getting dressed, when Rev. Guillaume, one of my colleagues, came barging in, panting and out of breath. He had to talk to me, he said. I was very much surprised to see him. Guillaume had used the wealth of his food packages to land a soft job as bookkeeper in an infirmary block. He led a relatively protected life there. He never had to attend roll calls, and he could get up whenever he wished, which was seldom before 7 A.M. Suddenly, this perpetual patient came bursting into our block at four in the morning, shouting: "Hey, man, you're going home today! Hurry up and pack your things!"

I have often since been asked, "How did you feel at that

moment?" I felt no joy, no overwhelming or boundless jubilation. My first reaction was, "Don't believe it! Don't get your hopes up until you are outside the gate. If it isn't true, you'll have an abysmal day!" To get over such a disappointment would take many days, and one could do without such disappointments in Dachau.

But Guillaume's information had come from the right source. When a prisoner was to be discharged, his name was given to the head bookkeeper of the infirmary. This was done the night before the discharge was to take place, after curfew (that is, after the camp streets were off-limits so that the prisoners were unable to get from block to block). The bookkeeper of the infirmary had to know which prisoners had to be examined the following morning before they were discharged. If someone were sick or in poor condition, he could not be discharged, for that might hurt the camp's reputation. People outside might think that the prisoners were not getting first-class treatment.

Nevertheless, although the news was almost certain to be true, I was still in a concentration camp, so nothing could be absolutely reliable. Therefore, I thought to myself, adapting Paul a little, I'll rejoice as though I weren't rejoicing, and I'll get ready as though I weren't getting ready. In other words, I wouldn't set my heart on it; I wouldn't count on going home too much.

But it was nice to get the news in advance, before the morning roll call. The official procedure was not to tell the prisoner until immediately after roll call, while he was still on the parade ground. Then he couldn't return to his block to pick up any of his things. This policy was designed to prevent messages from being passed out of the camp. Now I had a chance to get ready and to make arrangements. I had quite an inheritance to get rid of, for I had stashed away a substantial supply of food in my secret hideout to guard against bad times. I appointed Hinlooper as my heir. If he were set free before the end of the war, he would in turn choose another heir. And if he had to stay to the end, he would know how to distribute the supplies in the bad days that lay ahead.

I also packed some food and personal things into a box. Although it was strictly forbidden, I took a chance and carried the bulky thing along to roll call. I said my farewells to my friends—not an easy thing to do. How I wished I could take them all with me to freedom! Actually, I felt awkward and even somewhat ashamed. I hardly knew how to conduct myself before my friends, who were all staying behind. But they rejoiced, not only at my good fortune, but also because my discharge raised their hope that soon they too would be released. It was a joy, however, that was not without tears.

Immediately after roll call, just before the work leader yelled, "Form your kommandos," the bookkeeper of our block shouted, "Number 30650 step forward!" *Now* I was certain.

I had reason to rejoice. But I was still unable to. When an engine revs up too high, it stalls. That's how it is in moments of excessive grief or joy. There seems to be a limit to the amount of joy or grief that a person can experience. When this limit is reached, numbness sets in. When something is impossible to digest, it overwhelms you. That's the way it was with me. My joy was much greater than I could possibly express. But it was also subdued by the thought of the many friends that I was leaving behind. A quick flurry of handshakes, slaps on the back, some shoving and yelling in the middle of thousands of prisoners running to get to their work kommandos, and then I followed the bookkeeper to a venerable S.S. officer.

Two other men were also being discharged that morning. Both were German, and they were to be posted straight to the front, without being allowed to visit their wives and children. Nevertheless, they were unspeakably happy and thankful. Better, they said, to be free on the eastern front than to be forever staring through barbed wire. Only someone who has been locked up for a long time can truly understand the meaning of freedom.

The old officer first led us to the showers, where we stripped off our prison clothes and washed off the prison dirt. We were going to get our own clothes back. After having worn grotesque prison garb for close to two years, the thought of being able to wear my own clothes again was enough cause for me to celebrate. But I was in for a disappointment. The Sunday night before my discharge, we had been up all night watching the bombing of Munich—a fantastic display of antiaircraft fire and diving fighter planes!

The whole camp had been lit up by Allied flares. One of the flares had been hit by antiaircraft fire and dropped on the roof of the building where my clothes and those of other prisoners had been stored. The building caught fire and, although the camp fire engine soon extinguished the blaze, our clothes had been up in the attic. The clothes of prisoners number 1 to 36000 had been destroyed. My clothes were gone.

Therefore, I was given a collection of leftovers; a filthy, worn-out pair of slacks, a blue vest, and a brown suit coat without buttons. For an overcoat I was given a greenish jacket that was considerably shorter than my suit coat. I had to do without a shirt, collar, or tie. My big cardboard box and shoes without laces completed the picture. But I didn't care what I looked like. I was going home! Besides, I told myself, with a wry smile, the world is full of bums dressed like gentlemen. In my case, perhaps the world would see a gentlemen dressed like a bum!

The examination in the infirmary went smoothly. It was quickly determined that I could be safely sent into the free world as a living testimony to the loving care that I received in Dachau. I now weighed eighty-five kilograms (185 lbs.). Who would believe that only a few months earlier I had weighed less than forty kilograms (85 lbs.)? Who would believe that there had been days on which I had received as many as ten beatings? Those in charge of the infirmary could discharge me without a qualm. I would be living proof that all the grisly stories about Dachau were vicious lies! Just seeing me would be enough.

When we arrived at the administration building, I was filled with a sense of wonder. I had stood here a year and a half ago, studying the merciless message of the card system. Row after row of cards under the heading "Deceased," and only a few under the heading "Discharged." And hadn't one of the S.S. clerks assured me that in fourteen days I would celebrate Ascension Day by going up the chimney?

I had asked myself, how long will it be before my card is transferred to the "Deceased" category? It was just a simple administrative act. The record was kept up to date every day without any thought of human suffering. What difference did it make to the S.S. clerk if he had to transfer fifty or a hundred or several hundred cards from one category to another? At most, he might think, "Tough luck, fellows."

Here I stood—one of the "lucky" few, by God's grace. My card would be one of the few moved to the small "Discharged" column. I thought of all the friends and colleagues whose cards had joined the vast graveyard under "Deceased." But they weren't truly dead, they were alive! They had been discharged into a world where they found true freedom. In Christ the Victor, they had permanently overcome death.

I was treated with remarkable courtesy. The S.S. clerk said, "Today you have the great privilege of being discharged. It is our conviction that you have learned much during these years. You'll have to prove this out in the future. Your discharge is merely a test to see if you've really bettered yourself. If you show that you've learned nothing, you'll be sent back here to die in Dachau. You can show that you've earned your freedom by comprehending the new order of the great German Reich.

"Last of all, you'll have to sign a paper that you'll reveal nothing about Dachau, neither in speech nor in writing. This is to be taken very seriously. You may tell nothing, not even innocent details, such as whether or not you had to work or whether you lived in barracks or houses. If anyone asks you, tell him 'I know nothing; I refuse to talk about it.' " I listened

Konzentrationslager Dachau.

Kommandantur

Am 6.Oktober 1943.

Entlassungsschein.

Der Schutzhaftgefangene Jacobus O v e r d u i n

geb. 27.September 1902 zu Leiden/Holland

war bis zum heutigen Tage im Konzentrationslager Dachau verwahrt.

Laut Verfügung des RSHA.-Amt IV-Berlin vom 29.9.43 1VC2 - 0.3655

wurde die Schutzhaft aufgehoben. Er hat sich sofort beim Befehlshaber der Sicherheits-
polizei und des SD in Den Haag, Am Plein 1, zurückzumelden. Es wird gebeten,
ihm die Einreise in die besetzten niederl.Gebiete zu ermöglichen.

Lagerkommandant

Der Kommandant
Konzentrationslager Dachau
Nr 2

Lagerkommandant
Hauptsturmführer.

-7.Okt.1943

N/0073 4.43. 3000

to him with a meek and innocent face. And as I signed the paper meekly and innocently, I noted everything that the man said and did, so that I would forget nothing when the time came to tell.

Then I received my discharge papers, which gave me the right to travel home without interference. The old S.S. guard, who had stood beside me all the while, was given money to buy me a ticket home. So I was really free! I had papers to prove it! We walked out through the big gate emblazoned with the euphemism "Labor Makes Free." The heavy iron gates opened in front of me and closed behind me. But I had not been freed by my labor; rather, God in His grace had given me many faithful friends who had spared neither time nor effort nor cost nor risk to obtain my freedom.

I looked at the clock in the gate. It was a historic moment for me. I walked out of the claws of Himmler at 22 minutes to 10, on the morning of October 8, 1943.

It was a forty-five minute walk to the railroad station. My grandfatherly guard was very obliging and even carried my big cardboard box for me. Feeling like a gentleman accompanied by his valet, I strutted proudly along in my laceless shoes and hobo outfit. First, we had to pass through the large S.S. camp, past the S.S. barracks and other buildings. Last year, I had marched by here every day on my way to the place where we loaded coal.

There stood the big building of the S.S. Ministry of Finance—where I had been kicked out for laziness and insubordination.

Further on, I saw the railroad yards where I had suffered so horribly and also the place where I had worked unloading building supplies in the heavy Transportbaulage Kommando.

After passing through several gates, we came to the town of Dachau. I passed the S.S. street, where we had brought coal to the homes of the S.S. officers. There was the house and the basement where the woman had fled screaming from my frizzly skull. Once more I walked down the streets where we had tipped over garbage cans to combat the dreadful pangs of starvation with potato peelings and other waste.

That was all behind me now, in the past! I had lived through it all. How could I ever thank God for freedom! My heart was filled with jubilation, and inwardly I sang one Psalm after another. Slowly, an unutterable joy flowed through my being. It was beginning to sink in: I was free, I was going home to my wife and child, to my congregation and family, to my friends and my work!

At the station, the old S.S. guard bought me a ticket, guided me to the right platform, and put me on the train to Munich. As the train pulled out, he said, "Auf Wiedersehen!" (Be seeing you!)

"Not me!" I answered. His lips curled into a comprehending grin, exposing the brown stumps of a few wellworn teeth. That was my last picture of the Dachau S.S. It seemed symbolic. Much had changed in those two short years. What a contrast between my reception at the Dachau station and my departure.

I sat down. Alone. Alone, as a free man. No S.S. man behind me with a rifle. I cast an uncomfortable, apprehensive glance at my fellow passengers. I kept getting the feeling that one of them was a Gestapo agent who would approach me at any moment and rearrest me. I was awed by all these people who could step into a train and go wherever they pleased, without needing anyone's permission.

And I—I too was one of these wondrous beings who were not dizzied or frightened by the limitless possibilities of the freedom that they faced.

I arrived in Munich at 11:30, and I had to wait until 6:18 for the express to Keulen, which would leave from Platform 14. Although I could have sprouted wings in my eagerness to get back to Arnhem, I enjoyed the hustle and bustle of all the people at the station. I went and ordered a beer. From behind my little table I had a good view of the busy station. Just to sit and drink a glass of beer in freedom was quite a sensation all in itself.

After I had been sitting there enjoying myself for an hour

or so, the secret police began to take an interest in me. I looked like someone who had escaped from a labor camp, where many foreigners served as slave labor for the German Reich. Sure enough! Soon a couple of gentlemen, whom I had noticed looking me over fifteen minutes earlier, approached my table.

I was taken to an interrogation room in the station, and they ordered me to open my box. I was frisked and asked to show my papers. I answered that I had no identification, no pass, no travel papers—nothing. They thought that they had made a good catch. Then I triumphantly produced my discharge papers from Dachau, which safeguarded me against a new arrest.

By 5 o'clock, a huge army of women and children with all kinds of baggage had crowded onto and around Platform 14 for the express train north. I wondered how everyone was going to get aboard, even if it were an extraordinarily long train. The bombing of the last baroque city, Munich, and its many ornate buildings and palaces had begun. Many of its citizens were fleeing north to family and friends in the country.

But I managed to find standing room on one of the entryways of the train. I stood there for fourteen hours, until 7:30 the next morning when we arrived in Keulen. Even so, it was a good trip. The slight discomfort of the journey was nothing after what I had undergone in the concentration camps and prisons. Besides, I was on my way home. Again and again, I was forced to compare this trip to the transport that took me to Germany.

From Keulen to Arnhem, I could sit. Now I could see the damage that had been inflicted on this part of Germany. Allied bombs had wreaked destruction in Keulen, Duisburg, Ruhrort, Oberhausen, and throughout the area. We crossed the German border into Holland just before 12:30 on the afternoon of October 9. Emotions crowded in on me. I had left the hated land of the Nazis and had entered my beloved but still oppressed homeland.

Forty minutes later, the train pulled into Arnhem. My discharge papers ordered me to report straight to Gestapo headquarters in The Hague. While waiting for train connections, I was not allowed to leave the station. Therefore, I could not go home first and greet my wife and daughter in Arnhem. At every station where I had to wait more than half an hour for the next train, I had to have the back of my discharge papers signed by the station commander. But I couldn't wait any longer!

I had become so used to breaking regulations every chance that I got, I broke them now too. I left the station and walked into Arnhem to our old-age home. From there I could call my wife. One hour wouldn't make any difference. I would take the next train to The Hague. I rang the bell at the home. The housekeeper looked alarmed when she opened the door and a dirty tramp with a cardboard box stepped inside and strode upstairs. What a surprise for the director and some of the elderly members of my congregation!

They soon had the table loaded with all kinds of goodies, figuring that someone released from a camp must be terribly hungry. But food was the last thing on my mind. My only thought was to get to the telephone and call my wife. But she wasn't home! She was out of town at the home of Rev. Guillaume. The wives of imprisoned clergymen were having their monthly reunion. However, my little girl, who could walk and talk by now, was brought to the phone to say, "Hi, Daddy." It was the first time that I heard her voice. When I was arrested, she had been a little baby. She was saying "Hi" to a daddy whom she had never seen, as far as she could remember.

After the reunion, my wife planned to spend a few days with the people of my first congregation. She had not been at Guillaume's fifteen minutes when she received the unexpected good news. By rushing back immediately, she just made the trolley to Hoogeveen, which enabled her to get home at about 9 that evening.

Meanwhile, I called up my colleagues who just happened to

be together at an area meeting being held in Arnhem. A few minutes later they arrived at the old-age home to welcome me in my tramp's outfit. It was a glorious reunion! But it was high time for me to get back to the station to catch the train to The Hague.

Although I was dressed for fourth class, I decided to celebrate and travel first class. My fellow passengers eyed me suspiciously; they must have thought that I was a mental incompetent or some kind of petty criminal. I put them all at ease by saying, "If you'll take a good look, you'll notice that my face looks more decent than my clothes." They immediately understood my situation.

In The Hague, I went straight to Gestapo headquarters. After being sent from one building to the next and from one office to another, I finally reached the right place. I got quite a surprise when I reported in. I had expected a very cool and official reception, with another warning never again to say such foolish things against the German Reich. Perhaps, I thought, they would require a vocal or written pledge from me that I would not speak on certain issues in my sermons. I even considered the possibility that I might be immediately rearrested and thrown into a local prison. With the Gestapo, you could expect anything except logic or justice.

But the reception I got was totally unexpected. The officials who took my papers bowed to me as if I were a foreign ambassador. Other executives from adjoining offices were called in to be introduced to Rev. Overduin. They too bowed deeply. They acted as if they were welcoming back an old friend whom they hadn't seen in years. Everyone shook my hand and congratulated me. The mood was such that I wouldn't have been surprised if they had decorated me and broken out the champagne. Was I dreaming? No, I was just seeing another face that had been adopted by the nihilistic and opportunistic Gestapo.

As I said at the beginning of my account, the Nazis could show themselves in any guise, as devils or as angels of light. To put it differently, the S.S. was run by men who could be criminally insane, as they were in Dachau in 1942, or jovial, mannerly public-relations experts, as they were now. No conditions were put on my freedom; no warnings were issued; I was given nothing to sign. My wife was praised lavishly for her persistent fight for my life. Then I said goodbye.

But they weren't finished, even yet. The whole boisterous group of Gestapo officers came clattering down the stairs with me and escorted me out into the street, where they stood bowing and waving after me. The whole hypocritical display left me nauseated and speechless. I had to express my disgust somehow, but all that I could do was spit on the sidewalk.

I was now officially free. After dropping in on some of my family who lived in The Hague, I took a train back to Arnhem. I arrived about 10 P.M. This was the most wonderful moment of all! Finally I would see and touch my wife once again. We met on the same platform from which we had said our goodbyes a year and a half ago.

Out of the sixty-five men who had been with me that day on the transport from Amersfoort to Germany, there were at most five of us still alive. And I was one of them! It was a miracle! When we arrived home, the living room was almost buried under flowers and fruit and other gifts from my congregation, friends, relatives, and acquaintances. My little girl Trudy was, understandably, a little frightened by the strange man who had moved in. It took her several weeks to make friends with the newcomer who threatened her exclusive claim on her mother's time and affections. And it was some time before she started calling me Daddy.

Everything seemed strange and new to me at first. Everything caught my eye, and I could relish it anew: an easy chair, a table with a pretty tablecloth, a soft rug underfoot, my own books. But, above all, I rejoiced in my freedom. I could get up and go to bed whenever I pleased! I could walk out of the door into the street! I could hop on my bike or catch a streetcar!

The Sunday after my arrival was a day of celebration. In the morning, I celebrated with the East Church where I had

given my last sermon on "Blessed are those who are persecuted . . . ." And in the evening, I celebrated the Lord's
Supper with the West Church. To be reunited with my
congregation was a blessed and exhilarating climax to my
return, for they had faithfully remembered me and prayed
for me and for my wife during my imprisonment.

Fourteen days later I was back in The Hague for an inter-
view with the Gestapo official in charge of religious affairs in
the Netherlands. I wanted to talk with him about those of
my colleagues who were still imprisoned in Dachau. First I
conveyed my surprise at the enthusiastic welcome I had
received in The Hague when I reported in. For I had very
nearly been killed in the camp, and thousands of my
colleagues from all over Europe had died miserably.

The reason for my visit, I explained, was to plead for the
release of my colleagues. If the Gestapo were so happy at the
release of one man, the release of all these men ought to be of
even greater interest and benefit to the Gestapo. The officer
explained that the policy of the Reich toward the church had
been radically changed. A powerful man had arrived from
Berlin with the mission to make friends with the church.
Therefore, he confided to me, all Dutch clergymen would be
released, except for three men. One of these had been
charged with harboring Jews, and the other two with slan-
dering the Fuehrer himself.

All my pleading on their behalf was in vain; they could not
be pardoned. Nevertheless, I was very thankful for the
promise that the others would be freed. In October and
November of 1943, three more clergymen arrived home. But
that was all, until the end of the war in the Spring of 1945.

The Gestapo soon found that its friendship was not returned by the church or her ministers. On the contrary, almost
every minister of Calvinistic persuasion was engaged in illegal
work of some kind or another. With a few exceptions, all
these clergymen were involved in helping those forced to go
into hiding, and they urged young men to resist compulsory
labor service in Germany.

They also acted as liaisons between underground organizations and the young people of the church. And the Gestapo was well aware of this. Most of the underground workers that the Gestapo arrested or were looking for were active church members. After their arrest, when asked their religious affiliation, many a new prisoner heard the exclamation, "Another one of those damn Calvinists!" So the Gestapo soon gave up on its attempt to court the church, and the release of clergymen, of course, ended.

After a six-weeks' vacation, I went back to work. But I didn't get much of a chance to settle back into my former activities and into the familiar parsonage. A few months after my return, our house was seized by the Gestapo. Everything was impounded except our linen and my library. Into the house moved the hated S.S. who had already caused me so much misery. That was the deepest cut of all: to have those murderers sitting in our chairs, eating from our dishes, and sleeping in our bed.

Moreover, the Gestapo gentlemen in The Hague, who had given me such a hearty welcome, put men on me to watch my every move. Almost every Sunday, two plainclothesmen were in the congregation. The house was watched, and I was shadowed wherever I went. Not without cause, to be sure. From the Nazi viewpoint, there was bad blood in my family. My brother and my sister were both in prison on serious charges. They had both been threatened with the firing squad. If the Gestapo had known the half of it, they would have both been shot ten times over. I still managed to provide shelter overnight for underground workers who were passing through Arnhem. Occasionally, I received warnings to go into hiding myself, for underground workers sometimes reported that an order had gone out for my arrest.

Despite everything, I managed to carry on my work for several months, going into hiding every night. Finally, however, several members of my congregation were arrested and were repeatedly interrogated about me. I had just taken some time off, and the Gestapo was trying to find out where

I was staying. Thereafter, I stayed out of Arnhem, officially because I was on sick leave. But I had been classified as dangerous by the Gestapo, and Arnhem was no longer safe for me.

Dachau's Balance Sheet

I want to add a short evaluation, first looking back once more and then looking ahead. I would like to balance the books on Dachau and make a projection for the coming years. I shall be brief.

Under the most agonizing circumstances, with Death breathing down my neck and clawing my body, I never lost heart. This was a miracle wrought by prayer, the intercessory prayers of many Christians—prayers said in the churches on Sunday and prayers said at home at meals and at bedtime. I was deeply touched to hear that many people in my congregation had prayed for me every single night during the two years of my imprisonment.

You have to experience something as trying as I did to appreciate the power of prayer. Never say that prayer avails nothing. I am sure that there were those who waited for me who had moments of discouragement; for after all those prayers I was still in jail, and the news only continued to get worse. But those prayers were not in vain! Although I was not immediately freed from prison, God did give me an inner, spiritual freedom every day.

And, although I was denied the fellowship of my family,

my congregation, my friends and relatives, I received a much more important and enduring fellowship, namely, communion with Christ. God always answers the prayers of those who believe in Him and pray in Jesus' Name. However, quite often He gives us different answers from what we expect, and often they come in different ways and at different times from what we anticipate. But answer He does. Just because the answer is not what we expect, however, does not mean that it is less, worse, smaller, or poorer. No, it is always more, better, greater, richer than we expected.

Also, the prayers for those who died in the camps were heard and answered. They, too, knew the blessing of prayer. They experienced it differently, however, actually in richer measure, for they found eternal deliverance. Each of us received from God what he needed to keep spiritually upright—in a hellish life as well as in death.

The second thing that I wish to record on the profit side is the strengthening of my faith in the truth of God's Word and in His promises. After my release from Dachau, the Germans were still in power, and the Gestapo kept an eye on me, so I could not talk about what had happened to me. Yet, at a congregational meeting I spoke on "The Balance of Dachau," and I told of my imprisonment exclusively as an episode in the gracious history of God's Kingdom.

From a merely human viewpoint, those years were an oppressive nightmare, but seen spiritually they were a series of miracles of the Kingdom of Heaven. On the one hand, I was inclined to say, "How horrible that I had to endure all that suffering!" But on the other, I could never thank God enough that He had been so gracious as to allow me this experience.

Of course, I was already aware that God's Word was truth and that His promises are sure, simply because they *are* God's Word and God's promises and because God is always reliable and faithful. But to see the truth of His Word confirmed so strikingly in actual life situations is a unique gift of grace. Therefore, I was able to say to my congregation that everything that I preached in our days of prosperity and peace is true, wholly and completely true! God had tested that preaching by fire, but as the Gospel of God it is gold, pure gold. We can say with Peter, "For we did not follow cleverly devised myths."

The Gospel of Jesus Christ is no mere story, no romantic wish-fulfillment, no pipe dream out of touch with reality, no sweet lullaby from which we shall one day be harshly awakened. It is the most penetrating, the most powerful, the most victorious reality of all! It is not the product of human wisdom or piety. It is not something that we have artfully devised. It is the gift of God! We carry that Gospel into the world as a message from God. And everyone who truly believes in it will be saved—even if he is in a concentration camp.

God's Word is true because it is God's Word. That, of course, is primary. But, thank God that He also fulfills His truth in practice. God confirmed the truth of His promise, "Blessed are those who are persecuted for righteousness' sake." This teaching was also my strength when I worked in the Van Heutz "hostel" in Kampen, where the Dutch men and boys who had been seized in random raids were temporarily housed on their way to the forced-labor camps in Germany.

Many of them arrived at these camps more dead than alive. Many had spent four days and nights in the hold of some coal barge, without food and knee-deep in icy water, as they were being transported across the Zuider Zee. This was during the "Hunger Winter" of 1944-1945, and most of the men were already weak from starvation. The Van Heutz hostel was really an unheated stable; there were no bunks or mattresses, just a little straw on the floor. Hundreds, sometimes thousands of men, had to wait in this big horse barn for days, sometimes even weeks, to be shipped on to Germany. There was not nearly enough food to feed everybody, and no pans, bowls, or spoons for serving soup. The Red Cross worked hard, but it could do no more than pick up the seriously ill. The work was constantly hampered by the commandant and by the Nazi Mayor of Kampen.

I was once again reminded of the words of Paul in II Corinthians 1: "Who comforts us in all our affliction, so that we may be able to comfort those who are in any affliction, with the comfort with which we are comforted by God." My job therefore, was to be with these miserable slaves, to comfort and help them in their affliction—an affliction which I too had suffered for almost two years. God again confirmed His Word, so that I could comfort these prisoners with the same comfort with which I had been comforted. Therefore, God heard our prayers and softened the heart of the commandant, and he allowed me access to the Van Heutz hostel. I eventually received permission to visit there any time I wished.

With a staff of hard-working girls I scoured the city for small pans, spoons, socks, clothes, oatmeal, flour, Bibles, hymnals, books, magazines, writing paper, stamps, and other needed articles. What a grateful reception I got when I walked in and started distributing the things that these men and boys needed so badly!

Then I gave a short meditation and prayed with the prisoners. Afterwards, I set up an office in a corner of the stable to pass along messages from the underground, to help write letters home to wives and mothers, and to provide spiritual counselling. With the help of the Red Cross, over a period of time we managed to smuggle dozens of men out of the stable. First they stayed in hiding for a while with families in Kampen. Then, gradually, they found their way back home.

This work, too, God blessed richly. Some days I arrived at the hostel at 9 o'clock in the morning and didn't leave until curfew at eight in the evening. Again I was thankful to God for my prison experience, for now I could comfort them with the comfort with which I had been comforted. God's Word is truth. It always comes true. And that is how God enriches our lives. Then the torn clothes and bruises that we receive for the sake of God's Kingdom don't seem to matter very much.

I will always remember the faithfulness of the congregations at Arnhem and Kampen and elsewhere. Not just their prayers, but also their packages of food were of inestimable value to those of us in the camps. Several friends approached high German officials on my behalf. My discharge had already been approved in June of 1942 at a meeting of the Nazi brass. Gestapo headquarters in Arnhem, The Hague, and Berlin (Himmler) had also approved it. With such high credentials behind me, why hadn't I been released? Why was I kept in Dachau for another year and a half? This story again reveals the contrariness and injustice of a system that toyed with and wasted hundreds of thousands of lives. I'll give a brief summary of what happened.

At the beginning of June, when I was just being transported to Germany and had not yet arrived in Dachau, the commandant of Dachau had already received an order from Berlin for my immediate release. This was Commandant Hoffman, whose demented mind I have already shown in action. He had no intention of releasing any of his victims, especially if they were clergymen.

But could he simply ignore an order from Berlin? Easily, for if a camp commandant saw that a prisoner's attitude had not changed or that the prisoner had been reported for breaking camp rules, then he could decide to hold the prisoner for an undetermined length of time for offenses committed in the camp. Despite the release order, my future was in the commandant's hands. Berlin had done its duty; the rest was up to Commandant Hoffman.

Hoffman made use, perverse use, of the power given him and reported to Berlin that Overduin was behaving badly in the camp. Hence, the message went from Berlin to The Hague, and from The Hague to Arnhem: "Overduin has learned nothing; he is still a danger to the state." This was also the answer given by the Nazi authorities to Mr. H.G. Hey who came to plead on my behalf for the second time. He was told, further, that there was nothing more to be done. It was my own fault that I hadn't allowed myself to be "re-educated" (that is, indoctrinated by Nazi propaganda).

But at the time, Hoffman had never seen me, so he had no grounds for making such a statement. I suspect, however, that he may have been filled in by Berg, the commandant at Amersfoort.

In any case, the top Nazi officials said, "The Overduin case is closed. He is hopeless!" I was to be left in Dachau to die. This message was never passed on to my wife, lest she be deprived of all hope. But all her subsequent visits to Gestapo headquarters in Arnhem and The Hague were in vain. She was repeatedly sent home with empty promises, until finally one of the Gestapo in Arnhem told her, "Your husband isn't being released because he doesn't behave in camp. What's wrong with him that he has to be locked up?"

Normally my wife would have had little trouble listing some of my weaknesses, but to answer the Gestapo agent's question was not only hard; it was impossible. Then the Gestapo officer—Vande Brink was his name—advised my wife to urge me in her next letter, to be more obedient and industrious. My wife wrote the letter and sent it to Vande Brink for his judgment. She had a prompt reply: "Madame, your letter isn't pointed enough. You've got to be much more precise. Would you like me to draw up a model for you? Then you can rewrite it in your own words and send it to your husband."

The next day, Vande Brink's model arrived. It was *very* pointed. It went somewhat as follows: "It's a terrible shame that you've been in prison for a year and a half now. You can't do a thing for the congregation where you are; yet, their spiritual needs are tremendous in times like these. The people long for your return. Is it wise and right for you to be so stubborn and refuse to recognize the totally new situation that has come about? Aren't you obsessed with one idea? Surely the church is threatened by numerous other dangers that are even more important. Just think of the danger of Bolshevism! We ought to present a united front against the common enemy. Don't forget that the attitude of the occupation government toward the church has changed radically. It wants to join the church and Christianity in the fight against Bolshevism. Be smart and do whatever your superiors tell you, and I'm sure you'll be released in no time!" This was the letter my wife was supposed to put into her own words.

After my wife had read the model letter, she immediately called Gestapo headquarters and asked for Vande Brink. He answered in a very friendly tone, "'Well, Madame, what do you think of it? Good idea, wouldn't you say? That should do the trick!"

My wife responded, "I thank you for your trouble, Mr. Vande Brink, but if I write a letter like that, my husband will think I've suddenly lost my mind!"

Vande Brink didn't say another word; he just banged down the receiver. He must have thought, "Those pig-headed Dutchmen will never learn!"

Thank God, my wife and I never learned what they would have had us learn. However, I did get a letter from my wife in which she asked me to obey whenever possible and to act wisely. Such advice was never amiss.

Yet I puzzled over that letter time and time again. I could not fathom what lay behind those words. I was, of course, completely unaware of the efforts made on my behalf in Holland. I knew only that my friends would do everything possible to help me. What form this aid would take, I had no idea, but I turned over different possibilities in my mind.

Sometimes a clergyman was freed if he repudiated his calling. Very few took this way out, but an occasional clergyman could not resist the temptation. I wondered if this were what the letter was getting at. So I replied to my wife, "I don't know what you mean by being obedient and acting wisely. I mean to be both. But it is Jesus Christ who sets the limits. I am convinced that it is better for me to perish in obedience to Him than to win my freedom by being disobedient to Him." This ended the matter as far as I was concerned. But how, then, was I suddenly set free on October 8, 1943? I am not sure exactly what happened. But I am certain of two things.

In August of 1943, my wife did something that was strictly forbidden. She wrote a letter to the commandant of Dachau. She had no idea of course, what kind of perverse creature had been in charge prior to 1943 and what kind of man his successor was. Among other things, she wrote the following:

> In June of 1942 the authorities in Arnhem, The Hague, and Berlin said that my husband's release had been ordered. In spite of this, it is now a year later and he is still in prison. The Gestapo in Arnhem and in The Hague tell me that my husband is behaving badly. Would you please tell me in what respect my husband is misbehaving so that I can in turn advise him?

If the former commandant had received this letter, I would have been in terrible trouble. But it came into the hands of the new commandant, instead. What happened next I can only guess. Evidently, however, he did not lose his temper and fling the letter into the wastebasket. He looked into the matter. In my dossier was the release order of June, 1942, but also the "hold" placed on it by Hoffman on the grounds of alleged bad behavior. However, there was no proof of the latter, because I had carefully avoided drawing any official punishments. Knowing the kind of man his predecessor was, the commandant apparently grasped what had happened and immediately informed Berlin, The Hague, and Arnhem that there were no further objections to the authorization of the release order of June, 1942.

About the same time, someone in Arnhem persuaded an influential relative (whom, I don't know) to go to Berlin on my behalf. The response in Berlin was as follows: "We can't do a thing. It's a closed case. Everything depends on the commandant of Dachau, and he calls Overduin stubborn and unwilling to learn." So my unknown benefactor went to Dachau and took the commandant out hunting for a week, and eventually, tactfully, he put my case before the ruler of the camp.

This is all I know of the matter. Probably, there is some connection between these two events and my subsequent release. This whole series of events once again demonstrates that Nazi justice was extremely arbitrary and, therefore, terribly unjust.

In these days, the health and psychological state of the people are factors that can no longer be ignored by the governing body of a country, for one of the greatest threats to the well-being of a nation is the possibility of unruly action or even revolt by the unprincipled masses.

Large segments of the population in almost all nations are rootless and homeless. They keep running into reality and chafing under the changes of history in God's world. Life deals them hurtful blows, but they are not sure why. These people experienced the war years as an unrelieved nightmare, especially because of the ruthless suppression of freedom.

But the unprincipled masses could not see beyond the facts to the spiritual background. They could not read between the lines, just as they could not influence the course of events. They did not even see the war coming. Its tragedies and traumas just happened to them. Perhaps for a little while they even drew inspiration from the seemingly beautiful slogans of National Socialism. Like children, they didn't see the dangers ahead, and they became aware of them only after it was too late. By then the hard facts of the situation were already engulfing them and squeezing them unmercifully. Such persons have no foresight, and cannot anticipate events; they lack spiritual discernment.

A nation needs people who can look ahead and help to prevent a repetition of such events, in whatever form. The absolutism of National Socialism will not soon reappear in the same form or with the same name. But it will no doubt return in some other guise and with different slogans. Without moral and spiritual principles, the masses will be unable to recognize it in time. For they have no scriptural foundation; they are a shifting, pliable mass of relativists waiting to be shaped and led. Like potter's clay they can go in any direction, assume any shape. Who will be the potter?

To depend on an appeal to man's humanity is futile. What are the norms of humanity? Who has the final answer? The vegetarian and conservationist? The antichrist? The authoritarian? If man is autonomous and has the right to create his own norms, then every man must possess this right for himself.

Only by returning to the roots of Christianity, to the teachings of God's Word, can a nation and a people find security. We must act or refuse to act, not on the basis of our own will, but on the basis of God's will. The most principial resistance against the Nazi regime came from those who knew they had to keep saying No! for God's sake.

Every nation needs to be brought to Christ, the Crucified Savior and the Risen King. For He is the Way, the Truth, and the Life in *all* things. He is the only guarantee of the healthful development of the individual and of society, so that the people and the nation can reach their true potential. In Christ, God became man to free us from our inhumanity and to teach us how to be truly human.

A Dangerous Book

Writing this book was a dangerous undertaking. The decision to write came after a long personal struggle.

What was the peril that I foresaw? Actually, there were a number of dangers—for readers as well as for the author. On the other hand, there were several good reasons to yield to the repeated urgings of other Christians and of conscience that I write this book about my experiences as a prisoner. In this epilogue, I will mention the most important of those reasons before discussing the dangers.

My reasons for writing are these: We will never fully realize what a poisonous, destructive influence the degenerate principles preached by National Socialism can have on our lives. This I want to get across to you, and I hope I have succeeded. Moreover, I am convinced that the dangers in writing and reading "first-person" books do not cancel out their potential usefulness. The most important thing for us is that we focus not on ourselves but on God's honor and the welfare of our neighbors.

Let me now take up those dangers. They are the following: subjectivism, generalization, idealizing the past, repudiating the past, and finally the spiritual danger of playing the role of

242

a martyr, of seeking glory for supposed heroism.

First, then, there is the danger of wallowing in our subjectivity. This is an obvious danger, for it is extremely difficult to remain sober and objective after suffering two years of the most outrageous injustice and refined cruelty, sometimes open and brutal, sometimes camouflaged by eloquent but ultimately depraved slogans. It is nearly impossible to write about concentration camp experiences without letting passionate indignation and even boiling wrath become the dominant theme.

Nowhere is the basic dignity of man so deeply violated and mutilated as in a concentration camp, where the prisoner is without honor and without rights, where he is treated as human garbage, where he is "welcomed" by being told that he is worth less than the stones of the street. A stone can be used to walk on; but the prisoner has shown himself to be unworthy even to be used by others. He is worthless, a burden, he is told, and—worse still—a danger and a parasite to the world.

There were tens of thousands of well-bred, honorable citizens with good reputations who underwent such treatment during the twelve-year history of the godless Nazi regime. Because of this enormity, our contempt and loathing for such devilish brutality is so great that any reliving of such horrors through a book like this one tends once more to unleash our fury, rather than to excite our gratitude to God for His chastisement and deliverance. Also, is the attitude of holy indignation the proper one when we try to relate events in an objective and honest way? Isn't there a danger of exaggeration, of telling the story too much in terms of our human judgments?

To this I can only answer that anyone who tries to present the facts objectively cannot help being filled with anger. I would almost dare add that it is impossible to exaggerate the extent of the horrors of the camps; those horrors are beyond description and imagination.

Now, I do not mean to assert that each prisoner experienced each form of horror personally. Some forms of cruelty were suffered by all without exception, but there were horrors from which most were spared. Yet, seeing others suffer is often as difficult and painful as undergoing that suffering yourself.

In this book I have tried to let the facts speak for themselves as much as possible. But you must not be offended because I am unable to record those facts in the casual, objective language of a detached observer, a language wholly free of emotion and moral concern. That kind of objectivity would be a sign of spiritual death, a sign that the injustices crying out to God have made no meaningful impression on me.

Second, there is the danger of generalization. The story that I have told is about my experiences in four prisons (Arnhem, Essen, Würzburg, and Nuremberg) and two concentration camps (Amersfoort and Dachau, the latter about fifteen kilometers north of Munich). I do not mean to say that the conditions I experienced were duplicated in all prisons and concentration camps. Furthermore, the period of my imprisonment was February 8, 1942, through October 9, 1943—some twenty months. Even in this limited period of time, the routine of the camps was not always the same. In some months conditions were more intolerable than in others. I experienced the great turnaround in the treatment of the prisoners in Dachau around Christmas of 1942, a transformation which made us exclaim that Dachau's hell had become a sanatorium. Both these words—*hell* and *sanatorium*—should, of course, be seen as exaggerations, but they are also indicative.

Therefore, the tendency to generalize must be avoided. In the concentration camps at Vught and Amersfoort, there were better times and worse times, although I am convinced that Amersfoort was consistently worse than Vught.

Furthermore, we should not forget that the position of a prisoner in the camp did not always remain the same. Most of us were very poorly treated as far as bedding, food, and general treatment are concerned. But there were also the prominent and influential prisoners, who were given better positions, a situation that allowed them lighter work, more food, and better treatment.

Thus, living conditions were not the same for all prisoners. Not all the work assignments were equally taxing, and not all foremen or "capos" were equally cruel. This also applied to the S.S. men, who went along with the prisoners as guards, as well as to the prisoners in charge of the barracks (the *Blockältesten* and *Stübenältesten*).

The chances of survival and of achieving tolerable living conditions all depended on what sort of men you served under as camp commander, *Blockälteste, Stübenälteste,* and capo. Someone who worked in the kitchen or in the "hospital" did not have to fear hunger. There were extra tidbits to be had—more, in fact, than one might think.

In Dachau, the death rate in Barracks 4 and 6 was much lower than in Blocks 26, 28, and 30, where clergymen were housed. In Blocks 28 and 30, the *Blockältesten* and *Stübenältesten* were vicious. Mainly Polish clergymen were kept there and many died. In Block 26 treatment was better because German clergymen were imprisoned there.

Moreover, not all prisoners who survived have the same experiences to report. Dachau, especially in 1943, was a chaos of contradictions—the strictest regulations about certain little things, alongside great freedoms that prisoners could seize for themselves if they dared. The most horrible punishments were imposed for breaking the laws of the camp, yet there were all sorts of ingenious ways of dodging the rules. It may sound paradoxical, but that is how the camp was run. The trick was to disappear from sight in the camp itself at the critical moment.

All these considerations should remind us not to generalize, because not all the prisoners received the same treatment. Perhaps we could also speak of high tides and low tides in cruelty and suffering.

Third, we must be on guard against the danger of idealizing

what actually happened. I do not mean to suggest that prisoners might tend to idealize the prisons or concentration camps themselves, but there is a definite danger of idealizing the spiritual attitudes of prisoners. The truth is that by no means all prisoners were heroes who consciously accepted the possibility of martyrdom for the sake of their fatherland or for the Kingdom of God.

The camps, indeed, also held black marketeers, crooks, parasites—the bloodsuckers of society. There were also many who ended up in the camps almost by accident. They had always been afraid of saying or doing too much. They had been more than careful. Yet, through the impartial injustice of the Gestapo, they, too, found themselves in the camps.

Such people, who looked out only for themselves while they lived outside the camps, did not turn into moral and spiritual heroes once they got inside. Their stubbornly egoistic way of life continued within the camp.

These people were not a source of strength to their fellows. They did not help others, for they never forgot their own suffering for a moment. They spent their time complaining and they did not approach others in love to help them bear their sorrows. Self-centeredly, they seemed to think that they were the only ones having a hard time.

When such people also call themselves Christians, they do great damage to the cause of God's Kingdom in the camp, just as they earlier did outside the camp. Worst of all, they enjoyed assuming the aura of a martyr and receiving the praise given to heroes when they emerged from the camps.

We shall leave this group for the moment and look at others, those who *were* imprisoned for their religious convictions and bore their suffering in faith. Even of these it must be acknowledged that their lives in the camps were not always Christlike examples.

We get to know people best when we see them stripped of externals. A doctor once said to me, "We physicians know people best of all because we see them in their underwear." In a concentration camp, people walk around not in their underwear but in prisoner's rags. A prisoner can no longer hide behind a fancy, expensive uniform or the good impression made by immaculate personal grooming. His years of education and his university degrees mean nothing. It makes no difference whether he was a professor, a preacher, a doctor, or even a high-ranking politician. In fact, he is more likely to be scorned than respected for having held high office. The S.S. men assumed that anyone who did not work with his hands was a lazy good-for-nothing.

There was a hatred of anything remotely intellectual, a hatred arising from a deep-seated inferiority complex. Titles of any sort aroused a sick repugnance in the Nazis. The mere fact that someone had gold fillings in his teeth often led the sadists to kick their teeth out.

In short, values were transformed into their opposites in the camps. All intellectual achievements became crimes, except work performed for the Nazi party. People accustomed to politeness and decency were now exposed to snarling contempt and the most grievous abuses.

Not all prisoners could elevate themselves, psychologically, above these evils. After all, the purpose of the concentration camp was to break resistance, to smash anyone who dared to oppose the state, that great idol. The prisoners were worn down and broken in body and spirit. They were drained of the energy needed to say no. Any light that might expose the barbarism and gross sinfulness of Nazism had to be extinguished.

With many prisoners, the camps succeeded. Those victims remained broken men, living in spiritual darkness even after their release. In God's mercy, those who cracked under the strain were a minority. Most of the prisoners resisted the pressure, even though there were times of sorrow, depression, hopelessness, and mental illness in their bleak lives when their only future appeared to be inevitable death.

But that is not all that there was to the problem. Each prisoner was a whirl of contradictions, himself torn by inner conflicts. Great people sometimes acted very small. Heroism and petty-mindedness went hand in hand. Fearlessness and terror, faithfulness and unfaithfulness succeeded each other rapidly in the lives of the prisoners. Especially when they were engaged in the struggle for survival, in a desperate fight to hold death back, then deeply rooted evil urges and carnal inclinations could break through, passions that might never become evident in ordinary life.

No prisoner was spared such contradictions. The children of God imprisoned in the camps could also say: "The flesh struggles against the spirit. The spirit is willing, but the flesh is weak. The evil that I hate—that's what I wind up doing. Miserable man that I am, who will deliver me from this body of death?" To present reality faithfully then, we must not idealize the prisoners. They too were people of flesh and blood, subject to many weaknesses. Whatever anyone becomes or accomplishes, he owes to the grace of God, which is ours through Jesus Christ.

There is a fourth danger to consider, one that applies to me especially as the writer of this book, namely, blurring the past. It has often been observed that man lives between the past and the future, between memory and expectation, with the present a mere razor's edge. Schopenhauer, whose Christless view of life was understandably far from optimistic, spoke of our memory of the past in terms of regret and our expectation of the future in terms of anxiety. The present, then, was merely the continuing movement from regret to anxiety.

Those who look at life more optimistically, such as the Romantics, see life in the present as hanging between warm memories and joyous expectations. This outlook leaves us in a springtime mood, in the expectation of warm, sunny summer days. But it sees man as unfallen, and it denies both man's sinfulness and his need for salvation in Christ.

The truth is in neither pessimistic fatalism, nor in illusionary romanticism. The present is not merely caught between the past and the future. Apart from the tendency of youth to be preoccupied with the future, and older people with the past, we sometimes speak of the present as a new constellation that arises from the closing of the period just gone by.

For the survivors of Dachau, captivity belongs to the past and freedom to the present. We see that if a person has "nothing to do," he may be completely preoccupied with the past and keep reliving it in his mind, even to the point of becoming deranged. For such a person, the images of the past remain sharp, if not exaggerated. But if one is caught up in the stream of life again, with people making demands on one's time and attention and love and interest, one has little time to be occupied with the past. There is little place for the past in one's thoughts.

For such a person, the past blurs and gradually fades away. His mental images are no longer vivid. That is why I made a point of taking notes and telling some of my friends about my experiences, even during the time when such activities were dangerous because we were still under Nazi supremacy.

The past has blurred for me too, however, and therefore I was not able to "tell all." Yet, the activity of writing about those events has sharpened my memory and brought many events into focus again.

In the fifth place, I want to point to a spiritual danger—which is the most important danger of all—namely, that on some level, even unconsciously and unintentionally, we start to present ourselves as heroes and martyrs.

My good friend and colleague De Geus, who was released to higher glory not long after arriving in Dachau, always said "Let's make sure that we don't start relishing the martyr's role." What he meant to condemn is the kind of martyrdom that crowds Christ out of the picture in favor of the imposing, inspiring figure of the suffering believer.

There is, of course, a proper, a Biblical, concept of martyrdom. To be a martyr is to be a witness—at the cost of one's life, if necessary. But a true martyr testifies *not* about himself, *not* about his own piety, courage, and faithfulness, but always and only about *Christ*, about *His* power and faithfulness.

The person who points more to his own martyrdom than to
the One for whom he is permitted to suffer has no understanding of the secret of Christian martyrdom. For such a
person, martyrdom is an idolatry.

When I tried to tell you what I went through in my two
years of imprisonment, there is the possibility that you will
close the book with an image of me as a hero, while failing to
get any impression of Christ and His sovereign grace. There is
a great risk of robbing Christ of His honor when we talk
about our *own* experiences. Let us not underestimate those
deceitful hearts of ours.

To me it is profoundly significant that the last sermon I
was allowed to preach in the concentration camp at Dachau
(on the Sunday before I was let go on Wednesday, October 8,
1943) dealt with Luke 17:11-19, which records the story of the
ten lepers healed by Jesus. The ten lepers had much in common, but they were not the same in all respects. There was
one all-important difference.

The lepers had been driven out of society as unclean, just
as we had been forced into the concentration camp. The
lepers lived in a small world full of misery, just as we did.
They faced certain death, although one might survive longer
than another. Yet their life was a degenerative process headed
for death, just like our life in the camps. There was no
prospect of their ever escaping their plight through human
power—and we were in an analogous condition. There was
only one hope for them—Jesus of Nazareth, the Healer and
Redeemer. All ten cried out in their need and helplessness:
"Jesus, Master, have mercy on us!" And they all believed
that Jesus could and would heal them if they went to the
priest as He instructed them, to prove that they had indeed
been healed.

But here lies the difference. There was a principial
spiritual difference between one of the lepers and the other
nine; there was, in fact, a great gulf separating them. Two
people in similar circumstances do not necessarily have the
very same experience.

Nine of the lepers made their deliverance from sickness central. The Deliverer did not count. They were full of themselves, full of their recovered health, full of their deliverance from isolation, full of their entry into a new life with all its possibilities. What perspectives suddenly opened before them—work, family, marriage, friends, social life! But in their excitement they forgot the secret, the key, the cause, the *Giver* of their deliverance and joy.

They were soon back in their original homes with their families and neighbors, their health restored. The people stared at them in disbelief. For a while they were the subject of every conversation, the center of all attention, celebrities for a day. And when they described their healing, they did so that the spotlight fell on them, instead of Jesus. They gave the people who love sensation plenty to appease their appetites, feeding the superficiality that elevates secondary things above the things that count.

Only one of the lepers—and he was a Samaritan—saw past his deliverance to his Deliverer. He did not make himself central as a healed leper, but, instead, focused attention on Christ. Therefore, however much the prospect of a new future excited him, however much he yearned to see his family again, he first returned to Jesus to praise and thank Him. In his deliverance and restoration, this man saw Jesus first. The nine were concerned only about the gift (their healing), but the one was concerned about the Giver, the Healer.

This Samaritan must have given a much different report about *his* healing to his family, friends, and neighbors. And his report must have made a deep impression on them, for it was a testimony of the greatness and goodness of Jesus of Nazareth. But those hearing the reports of the other nine lepers who had been healed must have thought, "How lucky those lepers were! What an interesting story!"

At the time I preached this sermon, I did not know that I was about to be released. I remember clearly how I urged my colleagues and myself not to forget the story of the ten lepers, especially if God should show us the great grace of delivering us from our isolation, impurity, and despised status.

My sermon was addressed to clergymen only, for the only ones allowed in the chapel were the clergymen of Block 26. I assumed that if these men were ever released, a number of them would speak and write about their experiences. What a dangerous undertaking that is!

In our imprisonment we can only cry out, "Jesus, Master, have mercy on us!" We may even receive an answer to this prayer. But then comes the great division. Then comes the spiritual danger bound up with our deliverance, with the great privilege we enjoy. Then comes the temptation, the testing. Then we must show how we will conduct ourselves in the joy of our freedom. Will we talk excitedly about *our* liberation—or about our Liberator? Will we bow down at the feet of Jesus to thank Him for our salvation—or will we encourage people to adulate and honor us as heroes?

Casually we comment that the masses love sensation and prefer interesting stories to more earnest matters and the basic issues of life. That may be true. But we may be promulgating such sensationalism by the way we speak and write.

I concluded my sermon with the following prayer: "Jesus, Master, have mercy on us. Have mercy on us by saving us from the dangers of imprisonment, but have mercy on us also by saving us from the spiritual dangers accompanying liberation. Have mercy on us, so that we will speak about our deliverance in a way that our hearers see only You."

Now you understand why I regard speaking and writing about these concentration camp experiences as dangerous— spiritually dangerous. I hope you have not read my story out of a love for sensation or curiosity about conditions in Dachau. Keep the story of the ten lepers before your mind's eye as you recall the events recorded in this book. My prayer is that this story has made a God-glorifying impression on you, and that you will say with me, "How great and good Christ is, how faithful and merciful!"